THE
DOGS
OF THE WORLD

BO BENGTSON
ÅKE WINTZELL
IVAN SWEDRUP

THE
DOGS
OF THE WORLD

With 333 full-colour photographs

David & Charles

Newton Abbot · London · North Pomfret (Vt)

Front cover: cocker spaniel.

*The picture facing the title page shows a standard
schnauzer. Note that this dog has cropped ears. Although cropping of ears is prohibited
in many countries, regulations vary on whether dogs with cropped ears may compete
at dog shows*

Photograph credits: p 6 Visage, Jacana; p 7 Ministry of Culture and Science, Athens;
pp 10–11 (large picture) John Topham; pp 14–15 Jan Delden; no. 7, 27, 56, 57,
67, 70 Marc Buzzini; no. 52, 74, 75, 76, 179, 235 G.W.M. Smits; no. 194 The Pet
Library; 322 G. Lindgren.

Translation: Kristina Husberg

ISBN 0 7153 8431 7

© 1973 Swedish edition.
Interpublishing AB, Stockholm
© 1974 Dutch edition. Uitgeverij L. J. Veen
B. V., Wageningen
© 1977 English edition. David & Charles
(Publishers) Ltd
© 1982 English edition. David & Charles
(Publishers) Ltd

Printed in Spain by
Printer, industria gráfica sa
Barcelona D.L.B. 30179-1982
for David & Charles (Publishers) Limited
Brunel House Newton Abbot Devon

Contents

The dog now and then

Origin of the domestic dog

The origin of the domestic dog has been the subject of extensive scientific study. Research into this, as into so many other aspects of natural science, began with Carl von Linné (1707–1778), who in his major work *Systema Naturae* incorporated those breeds of domestic dog which he considered 'pure' in a zoological sense, ie clearly distinguishable from one another. In 1753, one of his pupils, Erik Lindecrantz (1727–1788), presented his own thesis in Latin entitled *Cynographia*. This work is one of the earliest attempts to describe a species of animal according to the methods laid down by Linné in his *Methodus Demonstrandi.*

The Australian wild dog, the Dingo, is considered to have been a domestic species introduced by man which later reverted to its wild state

Dogs of sighthound type hunting the boar are depicted on frescoes in the Mycenaean palace of Tiryns in Greece. The frescoes probably date from between 1400–1125 BC

In 1756, Lindecrantz produced parts of the thesis in Swedish, with certain additions. *Cynographia* or *Description of the Dog* (new edition 1962) contains not only a first attempt at a simple classification into breeds, but also descriptions of the dog's sense of smell, trainability, memory and watchfulness—all the qualities which originally made the dog of service to man and which we have subsequently increasingly developed and utilised.

Research on a wider scale began during the second half of the eighteenth century, when the German zoologist Pallas (one of Linné's many foreign collaborators, mostly active in Russia) and the Frenchman Buffon became interested in the ancestry of the domestic dog. In the mid-nineteenth century, when the Egyptian archaeological discoveries depicting dogs became generally known and after the identification of dog remains in the old Swiss lake-dwellings, research in this field got under way seriously.

Yet science has not been able to provide a conclusive answer to the question of how the domestic dog originated. There is no doubt about its zoological classification. It is generally agreed that, in common with the wolf, fox and jackal, it belongs to the modern dog family, *canidae*. But when it comes to establishing when and where, and out of which root stock, the domestic dog evolved, there are three possibilities: that it descends from the wolf; that it descends from the jackal; that it descends from a now extinct species of wild dog, of which no remains have yet been discovered.

New scientific discoveries

These theories have been put forward, more or less emphatically, by various writers, some pointing to one conclusion only, others combining the alternatives, ie that the domestic dog descends from a wolf-jackal cross. The latest scientific findings were reported in 1972 by the Finnish researcher Björn Kurtén (lecturer in palaeontology at the University of Helsinki) in *Hundsport* (no. 6/1972), the official journal of the Swedish Kennel Club.

The earliest known evidence of Canis is, strangely enough, not to be found in America but in Spain which shows that the species must have migrated from America to Eurasia at an early stage; the find dates back about 6–8 million years. Somewhat younger remains—4–2 million years old—in North America disclose an ancestor of today's prairie wolf, *Canis latrans*. There existed in Europe at that time an ancestor of the wolf, the so-called Etruscan wolf, *Canis etruscus*, from which, about 1 million years ago, the present species, *Canus lupus*, evolved. The latter subsequently became established also in the New World.

It is now generally believed that the domestic dog descends from the wolf. A previous theory claiming both wolf and jackal as ancestors no longer seems feasible. In fact, the wolf is the only member of the *canidae* family with both the intelligence and the highly developed social behaviour which also characterise the domestic dog. But when and where did the dog become domesticated? When did it become 'man's best friend', ie tame?

One has looked for evidence in south-western Asia, in the ancient cultures of Mesopotamia and adjacent areas. It was believed that the domestic dog may have descended from the fairly small wolf living in those parts as well as in India. Small pottery figures, evidently depicting dogs with curled tails, were found in the Stone Age village settlement of Jarmo in Iraq, the oldest dating from 6500BC. Fossilised bones have also been found although, generally, these would appear to be remains of wolves. Professor Magnus Degebøl from Copenhagen did, however, prove the existence of domesticated dogs in a British Stone Age settlement at Starr Carr in Yorkshire. This is dated at 7500BC, which makes it the oldest find in Eurasia. (A German discovery, the so-called Seckenberg dog from Frankfurt, is likely to belong to the same period although its age cannot be verified accurately.) Finds in Danish kitchen middens date back to the Stone Age, but these are approximately 1,000 years younger than the dog at Starr Carr.

All this would seem to indicate that man first domesticated the dog after glacial conditions ended, possibly around 8000BC. The dog would then have been the second domestic animal in our history, as domestication of the sheep took place earlier. Evidence has been found in Zawi Chemi Shanidar in northern Iraq that the sheep was domesticated around 9000BC.

Quite recently, however, new light was thrown on the subject by Dr Barbara Lawrence from Harvard University, who examined material from excavations in the so-called Jaguar Cave in Idaho, north-western USA. In these fragments she was able to identify teeth and jaw bones as having come from domestic dogs from a period of no less than 8300BC, ie almost 1,000 years older than the dog at Starr Carr. In addition, it emerged that two different types of dog were involved—a larger and a smaller one. I have subsequently had the opportunity of examining the fossils from Jaguar Cave and have been able not only to confirm Lawrence's findings, but also identify several leg bones as belonging to a domestic species. These legs bones all appear to relate to the smaller type of dog, the remains of this type being more numerous than those of the larger dog. By their different proportions, these bones are distinguishable from those of the wolf and prairie wolf which have also been found in Jaguar Cave.

These finds put a considerably earlier date to domestication than hitherto believed. At the time Jaguar Cave became a settlement, the dog must have been a domestic animal for a long time, probably thousands of years, as a division into types had already occurred.

The inhabitants of Jaguar Cave belonged to the so-called Palaeo Indians, a hunting people who established themselves in North America about 10,000BC. It is conceivable that they brought the dog from Siberia and that, therefore, the American domestic dogs may descend from stock which became domesticated as early as the glacial period in the Old World. These questions, however, can only be answered by new discoveries and studies. The same applies to the Australian wild dog, the dingo, which is believed to have been a domestic species introduced by man which later reverted to its wild state. We still don't know when its ancestors came to Australia.

So, much remains to be done to solve the enigma of the domestication of the dog. One thing, though, seems

The sheepdog's task is to gather the flock and drive it in the desired direction. It should also be able to find and drive back single sheep which have strayed from the flock. The most common sheepdog today is the Border collie

quite clear: that the dog must be considered the first of our domestic animals.

Dog meets man

One may assume that, through thousands of years, packs of dogs followed in the wake of human habitation, scavenging scraps of food. Most kept at a safe distance, but those bold enough to venture close to man and cunning enough not to get caught or killed, were also those with the greatest chance to find food, to survive and to breed. By discoveries of skeletons we know for certain that dogs were once used for human food. The bones have been well chewed by human teeth, the skulls have been smashed in order to get at the brain. Bearing in mind the abundance of game in those days it is unlikely, however, that the dog was primarily kept for slaughter but rather as a food reserve should the huntsmen return empty-handed. Puppies were frequently caught and adopted by women who had lost a child. Adoptions among the species are not uncommon and in certain primitive tribes the women suckle dogs as well as children. The dog is an animal very much governed by its sense of smell, and a dog which has been nursed by a women, and through her milk absorbed the human smell, easily identifies itself as a member of the human family.

It is unlikely that the dog's most important function was to help the huntsmen, as even the simplest forms of hunting require a certain amount of training, or at least a sense of co-operation. More probably the dog first made itself useful to man as a guard. To primitive man, darkness was the most dangerous enemy. At night, beyond the camp fire's circle of light, lurked dangers both real and imaginary—wild animals and evil spirits, the latter no less worrying because of their immunity to physical attack. It was here that the acutely developed sensory perceptions of the dog were put to use. It had soon been realised, no doubt, that the dog was able to warn of enemies approaching long before human sentries noticed anything. When the dogs suddenly stirred, hackles up and growling into the darkness, it was believed that they were able to see the enemy with their supposed 'second sight'—associated with the light patches of hair above the eyes which characterise dogs of a certain colour. To this day, there are still primitive people who consider these patches a most desirable feature.

Undoubtedly it was the dog's ability to raise the alarm against beasts of prey which was first exploited by man. Through its highly developed senses of smell and hearing in particular, the dog knew of the approaching danger long before it registered with man and so enabled the settlers to prepare themselves against attack. The dog's function as a guard was a fact.

As man acquired other domestic animals, the dog was called upon to protect these and to keep them together, thereby establishing itself as a shepherd, too. Ever since, the dog has been increasingly used in the service of society and the individual. Different breeds have evolved for different purposes and in many cases specialisation has been taken very far indeed.

Evolution of the breeds

More than any other mammal, the dog has branched out into a multitude of breeds. It is estimated that there are over 300 breeds throughout the world. Before the division into breeds began, a natural evolution took place in different parts of the world, creating types of dogs most suitable to their own environment and conditions. It is assumed that, originally, the dog was a comparatively slow animal relying not only on its delicate nose and hearing but also—and primarily—on its perseverance and stamina in tracking and eventually catching its prey. On the plains and in desert country, however, speed was the only means of escape for wild game when pursued by its enemies. In these circumstances, man needed hounds with qualities altogether different from those of the steady 'trotter'. A new type evolved—a rangy, long-legged, short-backed, swift hunter—relying more on its sight than its nose when pursuing its prey across open country. This type became the taproot of our present-day sighthounds which are fast but have limited staying power. When the borzoi was used in Russia for hunting hares—sometimes wolves and foxes—it was accepted that the hare would invariably get away unless the dog caught it within sixty seconds. This demonstrates that the dog was incapable of maintaining its speed for any length of time.

Apart from these naturally evolved types of dog, some breeds have come upon the scene as a result of mutations, ie complete divergence in type, which man has exploited by selective breeding. Such mutations are not uncommon among wild animals, but as these dogs are often handicapped in some way they usually succumb in the struggle for survival and disappear. For example, a mutation causing lack of pigmentation in a baby chaffinch makes it white instead of its normal protective colour. It then becomes an easier prey for its natural enemies and seldom lives to reach maturity and breed.

Useful mutations in domestic animals have always been seized upon by man who, by planned breeding, has established the peculiarity. These peculiarities have gradually been developed into breed characteristics. The dachshund is an example of a breed which originated through a mutation. In this case, the mutation affected the legs which became stunted at an early stage, resulting in what are now the characteristic short legs of the breed. This phenomenon is

Greenland dogs in the formation known as an Alaskan team. During breaks they just rest in the snow. They are used to never being indoors

known scientifically as chondrodystrophy. The bulldog, too, belongs to the group of breeds which has inherited chondrodystrophic traits.

By crossing the 'foundation breeds' with each other, new breeds have evolved making up a wide variety of dogs of different types and sizes—from the very smallest weighing a few pounds, to those approaching the two-hundredweight mark.

Division into groups

The attempts made in different parts of the world to evolve a systematic classification of dogs are neither logical nor consistent. Sometimes the classification is based on physical similarities or common ancestry. Some groups comprise breeds which are used for similar purposes. The efforts made in this field have proved that it is impossible to lay down hard and fast rules for a complete and consistent division into groups. The result is that different classifications are used in different countries.

In 1965, FCI (Fédération Cynologique Internationale) established a system, comprising ten groups, which is now in use in most European countries. These groups are:

1 herding breeds
2 guard/police/working breeds
3 terriers
4 dachshunds
5 hunting breeds (larger game)
6 hunting breeds (small game)
7 pointing gundogs (excluding British breeds)
8 pointing gundogs (British breeds)
9 other British gundogs
10 toys

The Kennel Club in Britain divides the breeds into six groups:

1 hounds
2 gundogs
3 terriers
4 utility breeds
5 working breeds
6 toys

The classification laid down by the American Kennel Club also consists of six groups, but with certain differences as to which breeds belong to which group:

The Alsatian is a very versatile working dog and, among other things, can be trained to search for missing persons. Known as the avalanche dog in some countries, it is often sent to find people buried in the snow

1 sporting breeds
2 hounds
3 working breeds
4 terriers
5 toys
6 non-sporting breeds

Since 1 January 1968, a common classification comprising eight groups has been in use in the four Scandinavian countries which, in spite of certain anomalies, gives some measure of uniformity to shows in Denmark, Finland, Norway and Sweden:

1 spitz breeds
2 trailing/hunting breeds
3 gundogs
4 guard/working breeds
5 terriers
6 sighthounds
7 non-sporting/companion breeds
8 toys

Dog shows and principles of judging

Nobody knows when and where dogs were first assessed by standards of physique. People have always had a need to appraise their domestic animals on a utilitarian basis, not least when culling their stock so that the number of animals kept would not exceed the supply of food available. It is likely that the first to go were the defective animals as well as those, including dogs, the owners could most easily do without. No doubt only the most useful dogs were allowed to live and breed in the early days of dog keeping.

With a more highly developed civilisation came the tendency to keep dogs for aesthetic reasons. As early as Greek and Roman times, dogs were prized for their beauty or unusual features. This practice continued among the wealthier social classes in all the European countries. The idea of systematically combining aesthetically pleasing characteristics with materially useful ones did not catch on seriously until the beginning of the nineteenth century.

The first dog shows

Throughout the ages, Britain has been regarded as the leading country for dog breeding and ownership and, not surprisingly, it was here that dog judging, in any real sense, was introduced. From the beginning the aim in Britain was to combine aesthetic and practical qualities in the dog, even if some of the driving force stemmed from the Briton's reputed characteristics—the wish to compete and the desire to bet on the result of a competition. The British have always taken a great interest in animals and the topic of conversation in country

pubs as well as on country estates would often be the ownership of the best looking and fastest horse. The latter question
was simply answered by a race, but the task of assessing
the visible merits was given to a few knowledgeable men
whose expertise was recognised and approved by the
wagerers. In time, dogs also became the object of betting—on
their ability to hunt in the shooting field, as sheepdogs or
on the finest looking animal. Someone with a knowledge of
dogs was appointed as judge, and so the foundation was laid
for our present-day dog shows.

The first dog show in the world was held, for gundogs
only, in Newcastle-on-Tyne in June 1859. The same year, in
November, another show was organised in Birmingham, this
time for a number of breeds: this event is regarded as the
first real dog show. Interest in shows grew quickly and soon
commercialism crept in as the breeding of show dogs became
a lucrative pastime. Because there were no rules and regulations governing the judges and their methods, corruption
flourished, dog shows got a bad name and attracted a purely
commercial following. Not until the foundation in 1873 of
the Kennel Club, which took responsibility for supervising
dog show activities, did the situation improve.

The original principles of judging and show organisation
were largely maintained, however, and even now people who
are considered knowledgeable are appointed to judge in Britain without any reference to their training and qualifications.
Nowadays, however, judges at the most important competitions—the Championship shows—must be approved by the
Kennel Club. The classification differs from the Scandinavian
one. Each breed is allotted several classes and one dog may
be entered in more than one class. The dogs are judged in
order of merit only: the judge normally places the first three
dogs in each class, with a fourth as a reserve. At some shows,
or in particularly large classes, additional cards are awarded
for 'Very Highly Commended', 'Highly Commended' and
'Commended' but these are not obligatory. The judge is not
required to justify his awards, but usually gives a brief report
on the winners indicating, primarily, their outstanding features. The British system, which is also used in America, Australia and most other English-speaking countries, makes for
very fast judging—a couple of hundred dogs per judge per
day is not uncommon.

Breed standards and methods of judging
To achieve more uniform judging patterns and to avoid the
danger of individual judges' preferences becoming too
dominant, the various clubs in Britain devised particular
breed standards outlining the features of the ideal dog in
the respective breeds. These standards, which were subsequently translated into other languages, form the basis for

Since man's earliest days, dogs have been used for hunting various kinds of game.
Opposite: *golden retrievers*; above, *spaniel*; below, *beagles*

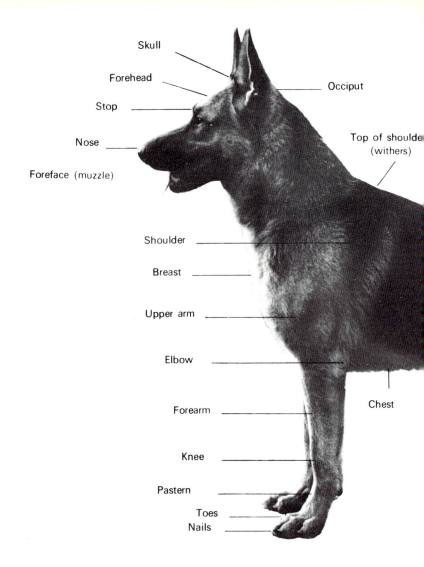

Skull

Forehead

Stop

Nose

Foreface (muzzle)

Occiput

Top of shoulder (withers)

Shoulder

Breast

Upper arm

Elbow

Forearm

Chest

Knee

Pastern

Toes

Nails

the judge's decisions without denying his right to a personal opinion where the standard is open to individual interpretation.

The interest in dog shows soon spread to the European continent, but judging there evolved along different lines. It was felt that the show results should serve as pointers to the breeders. There was not the same interest in the competitive element. It was less important *which* dog was the winner—it was more important to establish the merits of each individual competitor. Hence judging in Europe came to be dominated by qualitative assessment and the competitive approach limited to a few classes only—and these mainly for the entertainment of exhibitors and spectators.

The interest in dog shows has increased enormously in recent years, reflected in the number of shows and competitors. The general public's growing interest is indicated by the ever increasing attendance figures. This trend is apparent not

The anatomy of the dog

A special terminology—see the illustration below—is used by the judge when describing a dog's conformation to type in his written report.

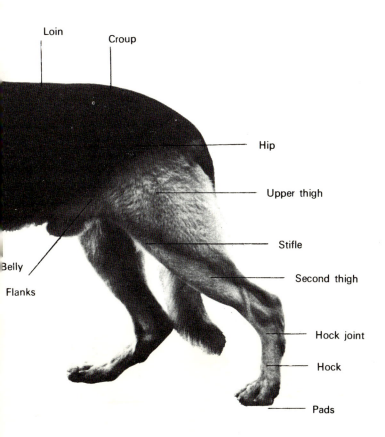

Loin

Croup

Hip

Upper thigh

Stifle

Second thigh

Hock joint

Hock

Pads

Belly

Flanks

only in countries like the USA and Britain, with a traditionally large following for dogs and dog events, but in most countries of the world.

The Continental system of judging, based on qualitative assessment, is used in Scandinavia, but in recent years more competitive classes have been added. It has been found that competitive classes are more of an attraction for both exhibitors and spectators than the often time-consuming and monotonous judging in the 'quality' classes. In a numerically large breed like the Alsatian, for example, the qualitative assessment in *one* class of *one* sex can take from four to five hours. Not until this qualitative judging is completed does something begin to happen in the ring—from the spectators' point of view—when the best dogs start competing against each other.

A gradual shift in emphasis from qualitative to competitive judging is likely if the present trend continues.

The Westminster dog show in Madison Square Gardens, New York, is one of the biggest and most famous shows in the world. The breeds in the row of pictures on the left are (from the top): Maltese, Chesapeake Bay retrievers and boxer. The boxer is a multiple Russian champion

The judge's task

According to the regulations governing judging at Scandinavian shows, which also largely apply in other countries, the judge's task is to assess and indicate through differentiating awards the quality of the dogs entered before him, as well as to place those dogs competing against each other in order of merit. He is also required to justify his decisions in a written report.

A dog show on these terms is purely a beauty competition, where conformation to the breed standard is the criterion. The dog should be judged solely on how it looks and shows on the day. The primary aim of judging is to assist the breeders by singling out in the respective breeds dogs of outstanding conformation and type. It is then up to the breeder to use this information, as well as his knowledge of the dog's breeding potential, in subsequent breeding. The dog show judge must not allow himself to be influenced by what he may know about the dog's performance as a stud dog or brood bitch, nor must he make any assumptions on this score. The exhibit should be judged not on its possible value to future generations, but simply as the product of previous generations of breeding. Individual merits as breeding stock can only be assessed through progeny classes.

In order to maintain the competitive element at dog shows, it is essential that judging is carried out according to clearly laid down rules and that the judge does not allow himself to be influenced by irrelevant considerations.

How to judge a dog

The judge considers firstly the dog's type and secondly balances good and bad points against each other. When assessing a dog's outline and type, the judge should also consider temperament and soundness. Correct type is thus of primary importance, the details taking second place. On this basis, a dog cannot be awarded a higher prize than its type justifies, but it could merit a lower one if the detailed examination reveals serious faults. It is important that the difference in types between the sexes is clearly distinguishable.

Movement, which is closely associated with the dog's type, must be carefully examined as part of the initial assessment. Movement is not an exterior feature as such, but a function of the dog's anatomy. Assessing movement, therefore, constitutes a check on the conclusions made when judging the dog's conformation. Putting a dog through its paces, incidentally, must not be done too enthusiastically as happens in certain breeds. A dog show is a beauty competition, not a race or a test of endurance for dog or handler.

The judge must pay close attention to a dog's temperament and general demeanour and carry out appropriate tests. These tests, however, should not be too forceful; in the show ring the dog should not be subjected to anything but the ordinary sights and sounds of normal life. Dogs whose behaviour makes judging difficult or impossible should be given a zero rating, regardless of their physical merits.

The judge's general impression of a dog is influenced by how it is presented in the ring. Fussy handling should, however, be discouraged and it is up to the judge to control excessive manoeuvring and if necessary prohibit 'topping and tailing'. The dog should be shown on a slack lead and, as far as possible, the handler should not touch the dog.

The way the dog has been trimmed should not influence the qualitative judging, unless the dog has been groomed in such a way as to make an assessment of its coat texture difficult or impossible.

Acquired defects may be forgiven at a qualitative assessment, providing these do not impede an accurate judgment. When dogs are judged in competition against each other, acquired defects may influence the final result, depending on how these detract from the general impression of the dog.

The dog in modern society

As we have already noted, in recent years most countries have experienced a marked increase in the public's interest in dogs and in dog ownership. In Sweden, for example, the dog population has risen from 196,000 in 1945 to about 400,000 in 1970—an increase of over 100 per cent in twenty-five years (these figures are based on official statistics of 'tax paying' dogs). Throughout World War II, many people were forced to get rid of their dogs because of the difficulty in feeding them during rationing. But as soon as the war was over the number of dogs began to increase rapidly. In Sweden there was an average increase of 15,000 dogs per year during 1946–50, while in 1951–5 it was about 6,000 a year. In 1955 the total number of dogs in Sweden reached the 300,000 mark for the first time and this figure remained fairly constant until 1959. Thereafter, the numbers began to grow again and during the 1960s the dog population grew by approximately 100,000 to reach the present total of about 400,000. As yet, there is no sign of any slackening in the growth rate of the dog population.

The figures quoted have been used to illustrate development in one country only, but there has been a similar trend in many other countries, notably in Europe and the USA.

Various theories have been put forward to explain the world-wide popularity of dog ownership. It has been suggested that the increase in dog populations in urban areas have been brought about by the city dweller subconsciously

Next page-spread: *An English setter in action covering the ground in search of birds*

regarding the dog as a means of re-establishing contact with nature. Another factor is the higher standard of living: more people can afford to buy and keep a dog. The increase in leisure time has also played a big part: owning and caring for a dog—quite apart from training it—can use up a lot of spare time for more than one member of the family. The growing prevalence of crime has led to more people acquiring dogs for protection against burglary and assault. Changing social conditions mean that more and more old people live alone with a dog as their only and closest companion—an aspect of dog ownership often overlooked. Doctors as well as veterinary surgeons confirm that in many cases a dog can provide a valuable psychological prop for lonely, insecure people. The dog is thus playing many important roles in our society.

Present-day problems
The developments discussed have brought a variety of problems in their wake. The increased number of dog owners has also brought an increased number of unsuitable dog owners who lack the ability or the desire, sometimes both, to care for their dog in such a way as to make it an asset to its owner and a pleasure to others. For the dog to be assimilated into modern, particularly urgan, society, certain conditions have to be imposed upon the dog owner concerning general care and training. Consideration should also be given to those members of the community who do not own, or even like, dogs. Massive efforts are needed in this respect by canine societies for the propagation of information on responsible dog management.

Hereditary defects in dogs are another cause for concern. These take the form of particular illnesses, mental deficiencies, etc. The increased demand for dogs has also encouraged unscrupulous breeders and dealers to exploit the situation by passing inferior dogs into the market at a good profit. What we need is firmer legislation to stop unscrupulous trading and more intensive research into rational breeding methods to help breeders to produce healthy, sound dogs. Above all, our aim must be to make more use of the discoveries in veterinary and other relevant sciences in order to maintain and continually improve our strains, to the advantage of the dogs, their owners and society as a whole.

Descriptions of the breeds

The description of each breed is accompanied by a colour photograph, either on the same, or on the facing, page.

At the head of the text for each breed is, where applicable, its name in English and/or the name of the breed in its reputed country of origin. The breeds are arranged in alphabetical order according to their names in the language of their respective countries. For practical reasons, some groups of breeds are listed together—for example, the terriers and the spaniels.

Breeds are listed in English and/or by their native names in the index; in some cases other names pertaining to a breed are also included. The numbers in the index refer to the corresponding numbers of text and illustrations.

1 Affenpinscher

The affenpinscher resembles a monkey, but in spite of this—
possibly because of it—it has never become very popular.
It is a very old breed and was depicted by Dutch painters
in the fourteenth century. It has always been regarded as
a close relative of the more common smooth-haired miniature
pinscher (124) and at one time was even considered to be
a wire-haired variety of that breed. Not until shortly before
1900 did the affenpinscher get breed classes at German shows,
but the breed has not gained significantly in numbers since
then, even on the Continent. Possibly the fact that it is
thought to be fairly aggressive has contributed to making
it somewhat of a rarity in most countries.

Its monkey-like appearance is perhaps largely due to its
round, black, lustrous eyes. It is a robust little dog with a
rounded skull, an undershot mouth giving it a cheeky expression, small pointed ears, a docked tail and a wiry coat which
is more abundant on the head.

The colour should preferably be black, but black with tan
or grey markings is also acceptable, as are other colours
except very light ones or white. Height at shoulder must not
exceed 11in, but the smaller the better.

Afghanistan

2 Afghan Hound

The conspicuous coat of the Afghan, its characteristic springy gait and, not least, its arrogant deportment immediately make it an object of attention and it is truly an exotic creature in our everyday Western life.

It originated in the plains south of Afghanistan, but in the bleak and rugged conditions of the Asian mountains it soon developed a protective coat as well as a keener temperament; there is evidence that the Afghan was used for hunting even big game in its native surroundings. The breed was not established in the West until about 1920, but then attracted enormous attention by its bizarre appearance and is now rapidly gaining in numbers in many countries.

The Afghan is dignified and strong and carries itself with supreme aloofness. The head is long and finely chiselled with a distant expression. The tail curls into a characteristic ring at the end. The coat is long and fine in texture on ribs, legs and ears, but short on the back and foreface.

All colours are acceptable. Height at shoulder is 27–29in for dogs, bitches are 2–3in smaller.

Morocco

3 Aïdi

The aïdi, a breed almost completely unknown outside its own home country, is excellent as a guard and working dog. Its origin is unknown, but one guess is that its ancestors were European mountain dogs which were brought over the Straits of Gibraltar and allowed to spread in the regions of the Atlas Mountains. It seems to be less common in desert country.

The aïdi is a powerful, bold and active dog with a piercing expression. When alert, it carries its ears semi-erect. The eyes are dark but may be any shade between black and brown, depending on the colour of the coat. This applies also to the colour of the nose. The coat is of medium length (about $2\frac{1}{2}$in), but with more abundant 'trousering' and tail feathering. In some areas in its home country its ears are cropped and tail docked, but this is generally considered undesirable.

The colour varies—white, black and white, fawn, pepper and salt and tricolour are acceptable. In particoloured dogs, a white collar is considered very desirable. Height at shoulder is about 20–25in.

Japan

4 Ainou (Hokkaido)

The ainou is one of the smaller Japanese spitz breeds, though not the smallest one: the shiba, for example, is an inch or so smaller and does not have the thick coat of the ainou. It takes its name from the island of Hokkaido, where the people originally bred their own variety of spitz. In many places the breed still goes under the name of this island. The ainou is used both for hunting and as a guard, but has remained fairly rare outside Japan. It is considered to be very easy to train, good tempered and affectionate.

It gives the impression of being a powerful, robust and yet very agile dog. The forequarters are more heavily developed and powerful than the rest of the body. The head is large with the characteristic erect ears of the spitz and orientally slanting eyes. The tail is thick and carried sabre-fashion over the back or slightly curled.

The colour may be red, white, black, black and tan, pepper and salt in shades of grey, red or black. Height at shoulder is 16–20in, proportionately less for bitches.

5 Akita Inu

The akita inu is also a Japanese spitz breed, extremely rare in other countries where it attracts immediate attention with its size, proud carriage and fearless expression. The Japanese regard it as their national breed and it is believed to be very old.

The akita inu is an imposing, bold and powerful dog with an alert expression. The eyes are dark, the ears erect with the tips pointing forwards. The tail is carried either gaily over the back or curled. The coat is short and straight, standing off from the body.

The colour varies from pure black to white and may be wheaten, steel blue or brindle. Height at shoulder should be 25–28in for dogs and 23–25in for bitches.

Alaska

6 Alaskan Malamute

The Alaskan malamute, one of the Arctic spitz breeds, is relatively rare outside the USA. It was originally used as a sledge dog by the native Alaskan people and was so suited to this task that it was soon used in preference to other varieties of sledge dogs. At the beginning of this century, it attracted the attention of the white man and became subjected to 'breed improvement'. Through interbreeding with other varieties, this soon resulted in pure-bred Alaskan malamutes becoming very rare.

The Alaskan malamute is a big, powerful, energetic dog, carrying its head proudly and moving with drive. The eyes are set obliquely and resemble those of a wolf, but maintaining a friendly expression. The coat is thick and coarse, particularly abundant on the chest, neck and tail where it forms a plume.

The colour is usually grey or black with white markings. Dogs stand about 25–28in at the shoulder, bitches 23–25in.

7 Ariègeois

This French hound is noted more for its stamina and sensitive nose than for its speed. It has been used for hunting in France throughout this century, particularly in the south-east (Ariège is one of the provinces bordering on Spain). Its background is genuinely French, being a cross between the old native breed briquet and the Gascon Saintongeois.

The Ariègeois is a graceful, elegant dog with a kind, calm expression. The eyes are always dark, the ears thin and supple but not excessively long. The tail is carried sabre-fashion, the coat smooth and close.

The colour is usually black and white with small tan spots above the eyes. Height at shoulder is 22–24in for dogs, 21–23in for bitches.

8 Australian Cattle Dog (Heeler)

The Australian cattle dog, previously always known as the heeler but now referred to by its official name, is considered to be a cross between collie, kelpie and dingo. Be that as it may, the fact that the breed earns its keep working the cattle herds is beyond doubt. It is an extremely efficient worker, alert and keen, and is therefore used herding cattle rather than sheep. The nickname 'heeler' was aquired because of its habit of quietly circling the herd and then, when necessary, racing in to nip the hocks of any stragglers.

The Australian cattle dog is always light, agile and active— never heavy or ungainly. The head is broad with a slightly domed skull and gradually tapering foreface. The ears are pointed, carried erect at a slight angle. The eyes are dark, oval in shape, with an alert expression. The nose is black. The body is of moderate length and strongly built. The front legs are straight with slightly sloping pasterns; hindquarters with hocks well let down. The tail reaches the hock, is well covered with hair and carried gaily in a gentle upward curve, drooping when the dog is at rest. The coat is fairly short and rough with a soft, thick undercoat.

The colour is usually a mottled blue with or without black markings. The head is blue or black and tan, and the tan should extend to markings on the forelegs, brisket and on the inside of the thighs. The colour may also be red-speckled with rich red markings on the head. Height at shoulder is about 18in.

Congo

9 Basenji

The basenji is the odd-one-out among the spitz breeds. Its country of origin is the Congo and it was not established in Europe until about 1940. It has, however, settled down well in its new environment and has all the qualities to make it popular as a pet—especially as, unlike most other spitz breeds, it does not make a nuisance of itself by excessive barking! The basenji is barkless and is only able to make squealing, yodelling noises.

In Africa, the basenji is used both for hunting and guarding. Despite its modest size, it is reputed to show considerable courage. It is finely boned, lively and graceful, moving with a swift, long, swinging stride. The head is characterised by the dark eyes, the typically wrinkled forehead and the pointed ears. The tail is tightly curled, set high and lies closely to the thigh. The skin is very supple, the coat sleek and close.

The colour is usually pure chestnut and white, but sometimes tricolour. Height at shoulder for dogs is about 17in, and about 16in for bitches. Weight is around 20lb.

Great Britain

10 Basset Hound

With its bloodhound type head on a short-legged, long and heavily built body, its long tail and jaunty movement, the basset hound is a breed which deserves a second look. It may not be everyone's idea of beauty, but its bizarre appearance in combination with its gentle, slightly melancholy temperament has made it very popular as a pet in Great Britain.

The basset was originally used for hunting in France, but became adopted by British breeders who crossed it with the bloodhound. Although generally kept as a pet nowadays, it is still sometimes used as a slow but skilful trailer.

Its most prominent characteristics are the soulful expression, loose skin and long, low shape. The coat is smooth and short.

Any recognised hound colour is acceptable, but generally it is tricolour (black, white and tan) or lemon and white. Height at shoulder is about 13–15in, and weight about 44lb.

11 Bavarian Gebirgsschweisshund
(Bayerischer Gebirgsschweisshund)

The Bavarian gebirgsschweisshund is less than 100 years old and evolved when the Germans needed a lightly built, agile dog for tracking deer in the mountainous terrain of Bavaria. Its main function was to use its sensitive nose to track its prey—other hounds took over the actual chase.

The Bavarian gebirgsschweisshund originates from the Hanoverian schweisshund (73), but has some blood from the short-legged hunting dogs which were also common ancestors of the Swedish drever and the dachshund. The two German varieties resemble one another in type, but the more recent, less common Bavarian gebirgsschweisshund is considerably lighter and more agile than its Hanoverian relative.

Height at shoulder should not exceed 20in for dogs; bitches are about 2in smaller.

12 Beagle *Great Britain*

Compared with the foxhound (58), which is rarely seen at modern dog shows, the career of the beagle has been meteoric and world-wide. It has much in common with the foxhound, however, although it is primarily used for hunting (hare) in packs, with the huntsmen on foot. Nowadays, the beagle is mostly kept as a pet—in Great Britain, its native country, in the USA and, increasingly, in many other parts of the world. In the Scandinavian countries quite a few are kept for hunting.

The beagle is compactly built and sturdy, giving the impression of great stamina and energy. The head is powerful without being coarse, the skull domed with a well defined stop (the angle between the forehead and the muzzle), the nose broad and the ears long and fine in texture. The neck is moderately long, well set into a noticeably ribbed, muscular body. The legs are straight, of good substance, round in bone and with well knuckled, strongly padded feet. The tail is carried gaily but not curled over the back. As well as the smooth-coated beagle, which has a short and very close coat, there is also a less common rough-coated variety.

The colour varies, but any recognised hound colour—which usually includes some white—is acceptable. Height at shoulder is 13–16in.

France

13 Beauceron
(Berger de la Beauce)

This fairly rare breed bears a striking resemblance to the dobermann, which is not surprising since it is believed that the berger de la Beauce contributed to the evolution of the widely known, but more recently evolved, German working breed.

This French breed descends from a very old, unrefined type of dog and was not generally seen until the end of the nineteenth century. Since then it has been vastly improved and is now easily trained and good tempered, although retaining its strong herding instincts.

The berger de la Beauce has erect ears—by nature or cropped—and a long, flat head. The eyes are dark in black-haired dogs but may match the colour of the coat. The tail is long and carried low. The coat is short and smooth.

The colour may be black, grey, red or black and tan. A small white spot on the chest is acceptable. Height at shoulder is 25–28in for dogs, 24–27in for bitches.

France

14 Briard

(Berger de la Brie)

The Briard has quite unfairly been described as 'one of Nature's jokes', although it is true that it is considered to be one of the 'fun' breeds. However, the Briard is an excellent sheepdog and much appreciated in its native country, where it also known as berger de Brie or chien de Brie. As far as is known, those few animals of the breed existing in other parts of the world have not been used as working dogs.

The Briard is tall with a long and shaggy coat. The head has a marked stop and the ears are cropped and heavily fringed. The long tail is carried low, the fringes forming a plume.

All colours are acceptable, but a dark blackish grey is usually preferred. Height at shoulder is 24–27in for dogs, 22–25in for bitches.

15 Berger des Pyrénées *France*

Although the berger des Pyrénées comes from the same area as the internationally known Pyrenean mountain dog, the two breeds are not thought to have a common origin. Both were used as sheepdogs, but while the Pyrenean was often called upon to defend the flock against wild animals, the main task of the berger des Pyrénées was to keep the sheep together. It is more closely related to the larger Briard and in most respects is just a smaller version.

According to the breed standard, the berger des Pyrénées is 'full of nervous energy' and very active. The eyes are expressive and chestnut brown in colour. The ears must on no account be carried fully erect (always a sign of mixed blood!), but should be so profusely feathered that they give the impression of being broader than they are high. The tail is bushy, set rather low and curls into a ring at the end. The coat is fairly short to long, always very thick and with a texture like 'a mixture of goatskin and fleece'.

The colour varies considerably: different shades of grey with or without black (and white markings on head, feet and chest), black with or without white, or even piebald. Height at shoulder is 16–20in for dogs, proportionately smaller for bitches.

France

16 Berger Picard

This French sheepdog from Picardy is said to have guarded animals in northern France since man first became herdsmen. Its origin is therefore fairly uncertain, but it has a lot in common with its Belgian relatives, the Groenendael (71) and the Tervueren (226), though the berger Picard is somewhat shaggier and less elegant.

It is powerful and muscular with an alert, intelligent expression. The ears are carried erect, the eyes hazel brown or darker. The tail curls into a slight ring at the end and, when the dog is in action, is carried in a delicate curve upward but not over the back. The coat is shaggy, but not longer than 2–3in and shorter on the head.

The berger Picard is usually grey with black, red or blue shadings. White patches, except for smaller ones on the toes, are not acceptable. Height at shoulder is 24–26in for dogs and about 2in less for bitches.

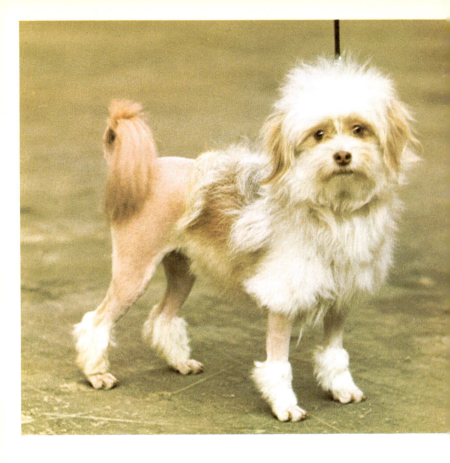

17 Little Lion Dog (Löwchen)
(Bichon Petit Chien Lion)

It is understandable that the little lion dog should frequently be mistaken for an unsuccessful poodle-cross. Its similarities to the poodle are, however, rather superficial—in both breeds it has been customary to clip the coat in a certain way. While the lion-clip in the poodle originally fulfilled a practical purpose, the aim of the löwchen owners has probably been to make their dogs look original and more 'lion-like'. 'Löwchen' is German and means 'little lion', and the style of clipping is to leave a lion's mane and tail tuft while the rest of the body is shaved clean.

The breed is believed to have originated in the French Mediterranean and is closely related to several other small breeds around those parts—the Maltese (99) is probably the only one better known. Although the little lion dog is probably several hundred years old as a breed, it has never become particularly popular.

The soft, profuse and thick coat may be of any colour. There is no specification of height, but weight is usually around 11–12lb.

Great Britain

18 Bloodhound

Nowadays the bloodhound is kept primarily as an original, wrinkled and good-humoured pet, but it is sometimes used to track escaped or missing persons—a task for which it is well equipped with its sensitive nose and ability to follow a trail accurately.

The bloodhound is now regarded as a pure British breed since it has been mostly used and appreciated in Britain for centuries, but it is descended from an ancient French hound.

The bloodhound is a large, powerful dog with a wise, dignified expression. It seems to be enveloped in a covering cut a trifle too generously. The head is long and narrow with long, thin and very soft, pendulous ears. The coat is short and usually black and/or tan. The mean average height at shoulder for dogs is 26in, 24in for bitches. Weight should be at least 90lb and 80lb respectively.

Soviet Union

19 Borzoi

By tradition, the borzoi is regarded as the number one beauty in the canine world—and not without reason. A good specimen of the breed with its sweeping lines is undoubtedly an extremely handsome sight.

The period of splendour for the borzoi was before the Revolution, when every Russian nobleman of note kept a team of his own and when the Tsar himself maintained a kennel of several hundred hounds. It had one purpose only— wolf hunting. Despite this, its temperament is now friendly, though not effusive.

It is a graceful dog with great muscular power and speed— one should not be allowed to forget its original purpose as a wolf killer! The head is of classical mould, long, lean and narrow with almond shaped eyes. The body is rather narrow but with great depth of brisket, the back rising in a graceful arch and covered in a long, silky, flat or curly coat. The long, elegant tail has profuse and soft feathering.

The Tsar reputedly preferred light coloured dogs, but all colours are acceptable. Height at shoulder for dogs is from 29in, bitches from 27in.

France

20 French Bulldog
(Bouledogue Français)

The French bulldog's many excellent qualities has made it popular with fanciers and pet owners alike. It is robust, steady and good-humoured and of a manageable size without being toyish.

The breed descends from bulldogs exported to France by the British and which subsequently interbred with various Continental toy breeds. In nineteenth-century Paris, the French bulldog became a thing of fashion and was bred fairly extensively, in spite of the fact that British breeders regarded it as a crossbreed. Nowadays many of the best animals are produced by British breeders which is proof, if any were needed, of the Frenchie's winning ways.

The French bulldog is cobby, well boned and thick-set. Behind its slightly pugnacious expression lies an outgoing and friendly dog. The body is higher at the loins than at the shoulder, but the front legs should not be crooked. The coat is smooth and lustrous.

The colour is brindle or pied; fawn is not approved in all countries. The weight is 17–30lb. Height at shoulder is about 15in.

Belgium

21 Bouvier
(Bouvier des Flandres)

A bouvier always attracts attention—it is rare, it is of considerable size and its appearance is distinguished. It bears a close resemblance to the giant schnauzer (148), but is even heavier and bigger boned. Like, the Groenendael (71) and the Tervueren (226), the bouvier comes from Belgium where it was used for herding cattle. Gradually the type produced in Flanders were bred. Not surprisingly, after World War II there were precious few dogs of this type left in its home area, and the bouvier has never become particularly strong in numbers.

The bouvier is robust and thick-set but still gives a general impression of style and presence. The coat is double with a thick, soft undercoat and a harsh top coat, particularly abundant on the head where it forms moustaches, chin whiskers and eyebrows which, according to the breed standard, gives the dog an unkempt look.

The colour may vary from pale fawn to dark grey, sometimes black and red particolour. Height at shoulder is about 26in and weight 66lb.

22 Boxer

Nowadays the boxer is generally kept as a pet. Usually out-classed by the Alsatian as a working dog, it is friendly, fond of children and much more playful than its mournful expression would suggest; it deserves its popularity.

The boxer has, of course, a great deal in common with the bulldog (28). In Ancient Greece bull breeds were used as fighting dogs but it was not until the Middle Ages that they were developed into dogs used for hunting larger game and eventually as sheepdogs. Towards the end of the nine-teenth century, the boxer evolved into a type clearly dis-tinguishable from a bulldog. The derivation of the name boxer is uncertain, but it is unlikely that it has anything to do with 'the noble art'.

The boxer is muscular, noble and clean cut. The shape of the head is its most important characteristic: the muzzle is well developed, broad and square with a slightly underhung lower jaw. The coat is short and shiny.

The colour is brindle, red or pied with a dark mask round the eyes and muzzle. Dogs stand 22–25in at the shoulder, bitches 21–23in.

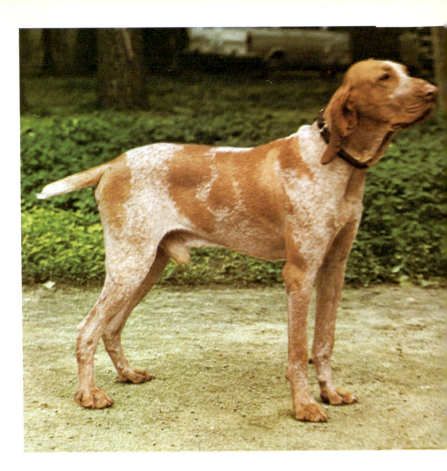

Italy

23 Bracco Italiano

Bracco Italiano, the Italians' answer to the Englishmen's pointer (127) and the Germans' vorsteh (49), is divided into two varieties: bianco arancio (orange and white) and roano marrone (chestnut roan). The former hails from Piedmont, the latter from Lombardy, but nowadays there are several intermediary colours and all these colour varieties are generally regarded as one breed.

The bracco Italiano is strongly built with a proudly carried head and a serious, kind and intelligent expression according to the breed standard. The nose is flesh-coloured or matches the coat in colour, the eyes are yellow. The long, soft and pendulous ears are fairly mobile. The coat is short and shiny.

The colour varies from pure white to white with orange or chestnut-coloured patches of different shades and sizes. Size, too, varies quite considerably—from 22–26in at the shoulder is acceptable.

24 Braque d'Auvergne

The French breeds belonging to the 'braque group' are
numerous and so similar in type that in many cases one
would prefer to describe them as different varieties of the
same breed. Many of them can only be considered as French
varieties of foreign, often more well known, breeds. The
braque d'Auvergne, for example, is very similar to the English
pointer (127) as well as the German shorthaired pointer.

Opinions differ regarding its origin—some consider it a
descendant of the old French braque which later interbred
with more recent breeds, others believe that it was brought
to France from Malta by Napoleon's returning troops.

The braque d'Auvergne is powerful, imposing and elegant.
The eyes are nut brown with a bold expression, the ears pendulous, long and smooth as satin. The tail is carried level
with the back and docked to 6–8in in length. The coat is
short, lustrous and weather-resistant.

The most desirable colour is white and bluish-black spots
of varying sizes and distribution. The head, however, is always
self-coloured. Ideal height at shoulder for dogs is 23–25in,
22–24in for bitches.

25 French Braque

(Braque Français)

The original French braque is believed to be very old, possibly one of the oldest hound breeds still preserved. Over the years it has contributed to the formation not only of many native breeds, but also of several foreign ones—the pointer (127), for example, is believed to descend from the French braque, even though the British considerably changed and improved it.

The French braque is a powerful, noble dog without appearing too heavy. The nose is chestnut brown, as are the eyes, though these may also be dark amber with a grave, affectionate expression. The loins are slightly arched and the tail, which is usually docked short, is carried in line with the back. Long tails are, however, acceptable. The coat is very short and close, and softer on the head and ears than on the body.

The colour is white with chestnut coloured patches and lighter or darker shadings. Height at shoulder may vary between 22–26in.

26 Braque Saint-Germain

The French braque Saint-Germain's close relationship to the pointer (127) is quite apparent; it is thought to have originated from a cross between an imported English pointer and French braques some time during the first half of the nineteenth century.

Although the braque Saint-Germain resembles the pointer, it is not as muscular or as heavily boned. The head is less distinctive than the pointer's, the nose flesh-coloured and the eyes amber. The tail is carried, like the pointer's, in line with the back and is not docked. The coat is short but fairly coarse.

The colour is white with bright orange markings. Dogs stand 20–25in at the shoulder, bitches 21–23in.

Switzerland

27 Bruno de Jura

(Bruno de Jura) (Jura Laufhund)

The bruno de Jura belongs to the group of Swiss harrier/fox-hound type breeds which also includes, for example, the Luzernstövare. As distinct from its close relative, the nieder-laufhunde, they are usually long-legged. Bruno de Jura, or Jura laufhund as it is sometimes called, is in fact not just one breed, but two. The breed standard particularly mentions also the St Hubertus variety which is more of a bloodhound type than the lighter, more common bruno de Jura.

In common with other Swiss hounds, the bruno de Jura is mostly used for hunting hare. It is considered to have a very good nose and a sonorous voice. In looks, it closely resembles its relatives: it is of medium size with rectangular body shape, a fairly long, narrow head with long, low-set ears and prominent occipital bone.

The more common variety of the bruno de Jura is either smooth or wire-haired. The St Hubertus variety is always smooth. The colour is fawn or reddish brown, sometimes with a black saddle, but there are a few all black dogs with slight brown markings. Minimum height is 16in, but 18–22in is average.

28 Bulldog

Although the bulldog is fairly uncommon outside its home country, it is probably more well known than almost any other breed and is frequently regarded as the symbol of the British nation. Its looks are hardly flattering, but it is an excellent choice as a steady, robust and original pet.

Its temperament originally was not good-natured. In the fourteenth century, it was used in the ancient sport of bull-baiting. The dogs had to seize the bull by the nose and not let go until the bull fell. When bull-baiting became illegal in the nineteenth century, these fierce dogs were in danger of becoming extinct. But thanks to a few dedicated breeders, the temperament improved so much that the position of the bulldog as the British national breed was secured.

The bulldog is thick-set and broad, slightly higher at the loins than at the shoulders. The head is large with a short muzzle and a turned-up lower jaw protruding considerably in front of the upper jaw. It has dark eyes and small, 'rose ears'. The tail is short and the coat close and smooth.

Colour varies considerably, mostly in combination with white and most varieties are acceptable. Weight is usually around 55lb; the breed standard does not specify height.

Great Britain

29 Bullmastiff

In many countries the heavy, impressive bullmastiff is very rare indeed, but in its native country it has commanded many faithful fanciers since it originated as a result of crosses between bulldogs (28) and mastiffs (102).

This cross is thought to have occurred several hundred years ago, when poaching was rife and the game keepers needed help against intruders. Being fairly uninterested in the wild game, the bullmastiff with its strength and substance was ideal as a mate on patrol in these circumstances. In spite of its forbidding appearance it was—and still is—surprisingly good-natured and rarely injured the poachers who were pinned to the ground by its weight! Not until well into this century did the bullmastiff gain official recognition as a breed.

The bullmastiff is massive and heavily built without appearing clumsy. The head is large and square with a short muzzle and dark eyes. The coat is short and close.

The colour is brindle, fawn or red with a dark mask round the eyes and on the muzzle. Height at shoulder for dogs is 25–27in, 24–26in for bitches. Weight is 90–130lb.

30 Canaan Dog *Israel*

In its native country Israel, the Canaan dog is used as a
sheepdog, as well as a guard and a message carrier. As a
messenger dog it is reported to have distinguished itself on
several occasions during the last few years of unrest in Israel.
The Canaan dog is hardly ever seen outside its home country,
the USA being one notable exception, where it has become
fashionable and is bred fairly extensively.

The Canaan dog is clearly of the spitz type and in character
it is noted for its suspicion towards strangers, plus a certain
tendency to roam and fight. If well treated, it can turn into
a very affectionate companion and an excellent guard.

The Canaan dog preferably has erect ears, but drop ears
are also acceptable. The eyes are very dark; lack of pigmentation on the nose is normal for particoloured dogs, and acceptable also for dogs of other colours. When the dog is alert,
the tail is carried in an arch over the back and is heavily
plumed. The coat is of medium length, straight and coarse.
Long- and short-coated dogs are acceptable but undesirable.

The colour ranges from sandy to reddish brown, white or
black. Common and acceptable varieties are particolour, piebald or Boston markings. Height at shoulder varies between
20–24in. The dog is always considerably taller than the bitch.

France

31 Standard Poodle
(Caniche Grand)

It is difficult to detect the original gundog in today's sophisticated show poodle, but those who believe that it has always
been at home in the drawing-room would be entirely mistaken. Well into this century, the poodle was used, particularly in France, as a water retriever and to scent out truffles.

Even now it is not unusual for a poodle to retrieve in
water and the often decried lion-clip is not just a fad of
modern breeders. When the coat got wet during a retrieve
in water, it grew heavy, so parts of the impeding coat were
cut, leaving those areas covering the rib cage, wrists and
hocks as protection against colds and rheumatism. The tuft

France

32 Miniature Poodle
(Caniche Moyen)

of hair on the tail made the dog easily seen from the shore.

The poodle descended from the type of gundog which was later the taproot of the harrier/foxhound and spaniel types. This relationship is discernible today, especially in standard poodles of the more old-fashioned type. It is easy to see that the Irish water spaniel (173) and the poodle are related.

A typical poodle is arrogant, very active and intelligent with good reach and proud carriage. The head is carried high with a fairly narrow skull and a long foreface with well defined chin. The eyes are almond shaped, dark brown and slightly obliquely set. The body is strong, muscular and not long; the tail is docked and carried at a slight angle away

France

33 Toy Poodle
(Caniche Nain)

from the body. The coat is woolly but not soft and thick all over; the lion-clip is normal in adult show poodles.

Colours accepted in all countries are black, white, brown and silver—but Great Britain and USA permit all solid, even colours, as do the Scandinavian countries. Regulations concerning sizes vary from country to country. In Scandinavia, the measure is approximately 18–22in for standard poodles, about 14–18in for miniatures and under 14in for toys.

The same breed standard applies to all three varieties, but generally speaking the standard poodle appears more powerful. Interbreeding between miniatures and toys is allowed and the puppies registered according to the size of the dam. Before entering a show they are remeasured and may be reclassified.

France

34 Pyrenean Mountain Dog
(Chien des Pyrenées)

A first-class Pyrenean is a magnificent animal, quite on a par with the Newfoundland (105) and the St Bernard (144). Yet it has failed to achieve popularity in some parts of the world. In many countries—particularly Great Britain—it is often shown in large numbers at dog shows.

The Pyrenean descends from south European herding breeds and comes from the border country between France and Spain. It is believed to have remained true to type during several hundred years without real intermingling with other breeds. Some time before the French Revolution, the Pyrenean had its moment of glory as a royal pet and a favourite at the Court.

The Pyrenean is a large dog with great substance and a kind, intelligent expression. It has a characteristic rolling movement and profuse, either straight or wavy coat.

The colour is white or predominantly white with badger or light tan markings. Dogs stand 27–32in at the shoulder, bitches 25–29in. Weight is between 90–125lb.

Mexico

35 Chihuahua, long-coat

The long-coated chihuahua was originally much rarer than the smooth-coated variety but is now very popular and of the same high quality. The breeds now have separate classification at shows, although interbreeding is permitted.

To the layman, the long-coated chihuahua may be mistaken for a papillon, but it is in fact identical with the smooth-coat with the exception of its long and soft-textured coat which is either flat or slightly wavy and particularly abundant on ears, neck and tail.

All colours or mixture of colours are acceptable in both varieties of chihuahua, which is yet another point of difference between the long-coat and the papillon. The long-coat, however, may be slightly larger than its smooth-coated cousin and can weigh up to about 8lb.

36 Chihuahua, smooth-coat

The chihuahua is the little dog with big personality. In spite of being the smallest breed in the world, it is extraordinarily full of itself. Part of the chihuahua's background was the ancient Aztec culture in Mexico, where toy dogs played an important role in religious ceremonies. They were burned with their dead masters and it was believed that the dead man's sins then left him and were transferred to the dog.

When the breed was rediscovered and the Americans became devotees, it was crossed with various other toy breeds which eventually led to its present appearance. It has become vastly popular all over the world in recent years.

The smooth-coat chihuahua is a neat, alert little dog with a saucy expression. The skull is 'apple domed', the eyes round, dark or matching the colour of the coat. Ruby eyes are considered very desirable.

Any colour or mixture of colours is acceptable. Weight should be up to 6lb, preferably 2–4lb. The breed standard does not specify height.

China

37 Chinese Crested Dog

The hairless Chinese crested dog is no longer to be found in China, but has primarily intrigued seekers after the esoteric in the USA and Great Britain as a canine curiosity. It is debatable whether the breed hails from China at all as its origin is fairly obscure, but it is a fact that hairless dogs existed in China, Japan, Africa, the West Indies and Central and South America for hundreds of years. The two most well known varieties are the Mexican and the Chinese.

The breed's most marked characteristic is its total absence of coat, except on the skull, feet and tip of the tail where it is long, fairly sparse and silky. The ears are erect or 'rose ears' and the general impression is that of a graceful, elegant dog. It is said to be very affectionate.

Colour may vary summer and winter according to the climate. It can be elephant grey, grey with unpigmented flesh-coloured patches or liver with grey or black patches. Weight is around 8–17lb and height at shoulder about 10–16in.

China

38 Chow Chow

The chow has a long and interesting history. Originally it came from China where, up to about 1000BC, it was used as a temple dog. Its purpose was to frighten off evil spirits and this is why chows with a severe, frowning and threatening expression were preferred. The breed came to Europe as early as the eighteenth century, since when it has been very popular as a companion.

According to the breed standard, the chow is leonine with a dignified bearing and aloof expression. It is active and well balanced but with a unique stilted gait. The head is large and broad with small, slightly rounded erect ears. The body is short and level, the legs well boned and straight. The tail is set high and carried well over the back.

There is a smooth-coated variety, but this is very rare. Normally the chow has a thick, straight coat, particularly abundant round the neck (the 'lion's mane'). The colour is black, red, fawn, cream, blue or white, never particoloured. Height at shoulder is at least 18in.

39 Collie, rough

For centuries, the rough collie has aided the shepherds in the Scottish Highlands, but it has not always been the elegant creature it is today. Originally it was an insignificant farm dog, one among many, but as the best ones were picked as sheepdogs the type gradually stabilised.

Not until about a century ago did the British begin to realise the merits of the collie. Queen Victoria kept and bred collies and encouraged an interest in improving them. Today, the collie's opportunities as a working dog are limited, but it fulfils—and very attractively—its function as a good-looking companion.

The rough collie is elegant and active, but also strongly built. The colour is usually sable and white, tricolour or blue merle (a marbled blue with white). Height at shoulder is 22–24in for dogs, 20–22in for bitches. Weight is 40–65lb.

40 Collie, smooth

The smooth collie is comparatively rare, both in Great Britain and outside its home country. With the exception of the coat, it conforms in all respects to the standard of the rough collie.

41 Bearded Collie

It is easy to recognise that the shaggy, friendly bearded collie has quite a lot in common with the more common rough collie and Shetland sheepdog, and the larger Old English sheepdog. Like these, its main function has been as a sheepdog, but while the other British herding breeds have not been active as working dogs for a considerable time, the bearded collie was, until only a few decades ago, exclusively used for work in the Scottish Highlands. A few years ago it was officially recognised as a breed by the Kennel Club and is already quite popular as a pet.

The bearded collie is active and strongly built without the massive appearance of the Old English sheepdog and, above all, without the enormous coat of the latter. The coat is profuse and shaggy without being too thick and is particularly abundant round the eyes and foreface.

The colour is slate or sandy with or without white. Height at shoulder is 20–24in for dogs, 18–22in for bitches.

42 Border Collie

The Border collie is not a breed in the official sense and, strictly speaking, should not be included in a compendium of the breeds as it has no officially recognised standard and no Kennel Club classification at dog shows. However, it deserves inclusion as nowadays it maintains a high standard of uniformity in type and it is also highly valued as a sheep-dog even outside its home country.

It is also difficult to decide the group of breeds in which to include the Border collie, but as it is used almost exclusively for work it would seem natural to count it among the working breeds.

The Border collie comes from the Border Country between England and Scotland. It resembles a small and very much less refined version of the rough collie (39)—the head is broader and coarser, the ears not as elegantly set and carried, and the coat not as profuse.

The colour is usually black with white markings and height at shoulder about 18–20in.

43 Coonhound, Black and Tan

The American black and tan is another name for this coon-hound which is the only one of the six varieties of coonhound which is officially recognised as a breed by the American Kennel Club. It is not often seen at dog shows, but is frequently used hunting racoon and opossum. As distinct from the other coonhounds, it is a close relative of the English bloodhound (18), though not as extreme in type. It also has unmistakable traces of the American foxhound (237).

The black and tan coonhound is, above all, an active, working dog. It bears a great resemblance to the bloodhound, but is of lighter build and lacks the folds of loose skin on the forehead. The ears are low set, long and pendulous.

The colour is always black with tan markings. Height at shoulder is usually about 26in. This may be exceeded provided the dog maintains soundness and balance.

44 English Coonhound

Strictly speaking, the name of the English coonhound is inaccurate—the breed evolved in the USA, but in order to separate this rarer version of coonhound from the others its undoubtedly British origin was seized upon in order to distinguish it. There is foxhound blood in its pedigree, even though this has become diluted in the USA through interbreeding with other hounds. The breed is not recognised by the American Kennel Club. The English coonhound is used for hunting in some parts—both racoon and other small game.

In comparison with the black and tan coonhound (43), the English variety is relatively lightly built and lacks the stamp of bloodhound. Height at shoulder is about 26in.

Yugoslavia

45 Dalmatian

Few breeds have such a varied history as the spotted dog, the Dalmatian. Nobody knows quite where it came from, but its official home country is Yugoslavia. There is no real proof to indicate that this is so and quite serious theories have been put forward that it hails from such divergent countries as Spain, Egypt, Denmark or India. Nowadays the inclination is to favour India as the most likely country of origin. Certainly there is some evidence that Dalmatians accompanied gypsies from the East during the Middle Ages.

Today, one would prefer to classify the Dalmatian as a British breed; it has been very popular since its first appearance in the British Isles in the eighteenth century when it was enjoyed particularly as a decorative carriage dog, running alongside or between the high carriage wheels.

The Dalmatian is an agile, symmetrical and muscular dog with active movement. The colour of the eyes depends on the markings and may even be yellow in liver spotted dogs.

Colour and markings are its most prominent characteristics. The ideal Dalmatian is evenly marked all over with small round black or liver spots. Height at shoulder is 20in.

46 Great Dane (Deutsche Dogge)

The heavy mastiff-type dogs used by the Romans in warfare are an ancient breed, whereas their more elegant descendant, the great Dane, did not get its present-day looks until comparatively recently.

To Continental noblemen who laid the foundations of the breed used it primarily for hunting. The older bull breeds were too heavy and slow to be really efficient for hunting larger game, so blood from the largest, heaviest sighthounds was introduced at an early stage. The breed is thought in some quarters to have originated in Denmark but the Germans have just as strong a claim, as they were for a long time the leading breeders.

The ideal great Dane is the perfect combination of strength and elegance. The proudly carried head is broad and deep viewed from the side, with a pronounced stop and a deep muzzle. The ears are carried close to the head or cropped, according to the regulations of the country. The coat is short and sleek.

The colour may be fawn, black, blue, brindle or piebald. Dogs should preferably be well above the minimum height at shoulder of 30in. Corresponding height for bitches is 28in.

47 Alsatian (German Shepherd Dog)
(Deutscher Schäferhund)

Nowadays, the Alsatian is probably the most internationally popular breed. It is the working dog above all others, but what makes it ideally suited to training in a variety of fields makes it equally unsuitable in the wrong hands. Also, because of its general popularity, the breed has often suffered through activities of unscrupulous breeders and dealers—sometimes with a deterioration in temperament as well as conformation as a result.

The Alsatian did not become a breed in the real sense until the latter half of the nineteenth century, and the way it looks today is the result of only a few decades of intensive and skilful German breeding. Predominantly native breeds form the foundation of the Alsatian—from pure spitz breed types to dogs on sheepdog lines. These, however, were soon transformed by the Germans' thorough and strongly centrally directed breeding methods.

According to the breed standard, the Alsatian is active, alert and good-natured. The colour is usually shades of grey to black with even, lighter markings. Height at shoulder for dogs is 24–26in, 22–24in for bitches.

48 German Wirehaired Pointer
(Deutscher Vorstehhund, Drahthaar)

Although the German wirehaired pointer is exactly like the shorthaired variety, apart from the coat, it has a somewhat different background. Wirehaired German gundogs are mentioned in medieval literature, but not until this century were German wirehaired pointers recognised as a breed. One reason for this was that until then it had been divided into many different types competing against each other to find favour with the hunters. It is also believed that the English pointer (127) may have contributed to the breed, although not as much as to the German shorthaired pointer (49).

With the exception of the coat, the German wirehaired pointer conforms to the standard of the shorthaired variety. The coat, however, is rough and close all over except on the ears, eyebrows and jaws where it is more profuse.

49 German Shorthaired Pointer *Germany*
(Deutscher Vorstehhund, Kurzhaar)

The German shorthaired pointer is the Germans' answer to the Englishmen's pointer (127), though it is largely thanks to the English pointer that the German breed exists at all.

The foundations are the same: imported French and Spanish gundogs. In England the pointer got a dash of foxhound (58), while the German pointing gundogs were crossed with heavy and unsuitable breeds—even bull breeds—and soon lost a great deal of their usefulness in the field. In the middle of the nineteenth century, shorthaired gundogs were therefore imported and interbreeding with these pointers produced a less extreme but all-round working gundog which became the present German shorthaired pointer.

A German shorthaired pointer is classy without being too elegant, and powerful without being too heavy. The ears are soft and hang close to the head, the nose is solid brown. The back is slightly sloping, the chest well developed and the legs muscular with well bent stifles. The tail is docked to medium length—about two thirds from the root. The coat is thick and short but fairly coarse.

The colour is liver, liver and white spotted or liver and white ticked. Dogs stand 23–25in at the shoulder, bitches 21–23in.

50 Dobermann
(Dobermann Pinscher)

A first-class Dobermann is one of the most handsome creatures in the canine world. Breeders originally aimed at producing dogs with as sharp a temperament as possible, but these traits have become less defined during the past few decades.

Most of the working breeds, however recently-acquired their present-day looks might be, have fairly long histories. Not so the Dobermann. It is named after the German dog-catcher Dobermann, who at the turn of this century used some of his stray dogs to breed as mean and as vicious a dog as possible. Conformation was of secondary importance, but as far as temperament was concerned he succeeded beyond expectation. After Dobermann's time, the breed was crossed with, among others, Manchester terriers (214) and greyhounds (64) and has since improved in conformation and become more manageable in temperament.

The Dobermann is a clean-cut, powerful and elegant dog. The colour is black or liver brown with tan markings. Dogs stand about 26in at the shoulder, bitches about 25in. Weight is around 55lb.

France

51 Dogue de Bordeaux

Separate classification of the great variety of similar mastiff-type breeds in existence might appear to be unjustified to some people: the difference between the English bullmastiff (29) and the French dogue de Bordeaux, for instance, may be apparent to those with a trained eye, but to the layman the two breeds probably look identical.

The dogue de Bordeaux is comparatively rare even in its home country and is practically never seen outside it. Considered to be rather sulky and moody in temperament, it is a fairly heavy, thickset dog with a large, broad head and a proud expression. The nose is usually dark but may be lighter in dogs with a tan mask. The eyes are large, set wide apart but never protruding. The tail is carried low except when the dog is in action when it may be carried in line with the back. The coat is smooth and short.

Warm self-coloured mahogany, golden or grey are the most desirable colours. Height at shoulder varies from 23–26in, with bitches proportionately smaller. The weight may be up to about 100lb.

Holland

52 Drentse Patrijshond

The drentse patrijshond is a breed little known outside its Dutch home ground, but it is reputed to be excellent not only as a pointing gundog but also as a water retriever. Its adaptability and intelligence also make it a nice pet.

The coat is very thick and of medium length on the body, longer around the neck and chest and with long, wavy fringes on ears and tail.

The colour is white with brown or orange patches. The official breed standard does not specify size, but a mean shoulder height of 24in would be average.

Sweden

53 Drever

Nowadays the drever is looked upon as a thoroughly Swedish breed, but in fact it originated in Germany; originally, most of the dogs were imported by a German living in Sweden at the beginning of this century. In those days it was known as the dachsbracke and it was not until 1947 that the German name was replaced by the Swedish drever. A few years later, the drever was officially recognised as a breed.

Although practically every drever in Sweden is used at times for hunting, the breed is still one of the largest in numbers in the country, with an annual registration figure of two thousand. Outside Sweden, it has really gained ground only in Finland, Norway and Denmark. In Denmark it has been bred for a long time under the name of strellufsstövare.

The drever is robust, sturdily built and well–knit, despite its long body. It is docile but alert.

The colour is usually a reddish fawn with white markings, or black with white and/or tan markings. A white blaze and a white collar are desirable. Height at shoulder for dogs is 13–15in, 12–14in for bitches.

France

54 Brittany Spaniel (Epagneul Breton)

Despite its name, the modern Brittany spaniel can claim that America almost as much as France is its country of origin. The French were first to produce the original true-to-type dogs in the middle of the nineteenth century and started using the breed as a pointing gundog, but it was not generally known outside its home country until the Americans adopted it and enthusiastically displayed its virtues to the world.

It was not long before Brittany spaniels were exported— from the USA as much as from France—to many different countries and the breed is now represented all over the world.

It is quite apparent that the Brittany spaniel is related to the old types of working spaniel which were imported into France from Great Britain. It is symmetrically built and on the same lines as modern English spaniels without being too extreme in type. The head is fairly broad, the ears are higher set than those of a cocker spaniel and it is shorter in neck but longer in body and higher on the leg. The tail is short or non-existent. The coat is thick and soft, but not too profuse, except on ears, belly and breeches where it forms attractive fringes.

The colour is white with dark orange markings. Height at shoulder is about 20in.

55 French Spaniel
(Epagneul Français)

The French spaniel may not be as well known outside its own country as its British cousins, but it is just as old. Basically it comes from the same family, but in the course of time, isolated from other types of spaniel, the French spaniel has developed its own characteristics. In conformation it now resembles a cross between the English springer spaniel (171) and the Cavalier King Charles spaniel (168).

The French spaniel is plainer in head than, say, the cocker spaniel (170) but is still very much of spaniel type. The ears are set fairly high, the eyes are dark amber in colour with an extremely kind and intelligent expression. The tail is not docked, but fairly long and is carried low or in line with the back in a gentle S-shape. The coat is soft and abundant, slightly wavy and well feathered on ears and tail.

The colour is always white with chestnut markings. Average height at shoulder for dogs is about 22–24in, bitches 21–23in. There is an allowance of about an inch or so above or below these measures.

56 Epagneul de Pont Audemère

This breed of spaniel, rare even in its home country, is said to be descended from a cross between the common old French spaniel and the Irish water spaniel (173). In appearance, the epagneul de Pont Audemère generally resembles the latter although it is not quite as profusely coated.

It has a brown nose, dark amber-coloured eyes, docked tail and a thick, slightly wavy but close coat.

The colour is chestnut with or without grey markings. Height at shoulder varies between 20–23in.

57 Fauve de Bretagne, Basset

The basset from Brittany originates from a larger breed of griffon crossed with more short-legged varieties of basset, one of which is the basset griffon Vendéen. It is built for hunting in rough terrain and, though much smaller in stature than its ancestors, has maintained most of their characteristics.

The basset fauve de Bretagne is active and fast for its size. Its body shape is rectangular with very heavy bone. The foreface is straight or very slightly convex, the occipital bone prominent. The eyes are dark without revealing the inner eyelid. The ears are large and pendulous, the neck muscular and fairly short. The coat is very rough and close.

The colour is either wheaten or grey, preferably without markings on chest and feet. Height at shoulder varies between 13–14in.

58 Foxhound

Although the English foxhound is bred with the greatest care and records and registration details are immaculately kept, the Kennel Club of Great Britain never provides classes for foxhounds at dog shows. The reason for this is reputed to be the British determination to preserve the foxhound as a pure working breed, and as such it is world renowned—most people have seen paintings and photographs of English fox hunts with a pack of hounds in full cry over the hills. Hounds exported from Britain in recent years have, however, been shown in some countries.

As looks are of secondary importance to working abilities, breed type varies a great deal. The colour is usually tan with a black saddle and white markings on the foreface, chest, belly, legs and tail, or white with black, tan or lemon markings. Height at shoulder is about 24in.

59 Old Danish Hönsehund *Denmark*
(Gammel Dansk Hönsehund)

The terrain of Denmark provides conditions which are most suitable for hunting with pointing gundogs and the Danes have evolved their own breed of gundog, the Old Danish hönsehund, which dates back about two hundred years. Its foundations were laid as early as the beginning of the eighteenth century through crosses between roaming gypsy dogs and local farm dogs. Quite a dash of bloodhound (18) is also thought to have contributed to the combination and these traits are apparent even today. Not until 1960 did the Danish Kennel Club recognise the breed.

One of the most typical points of the breed is the marked difference between the dog and bitch: the dog is impressively heavy and massive, while the bitch is considerably lighter and more active. The head is fairly large and broad with prominent occiput, the eyes—like the bloodhound's—sometimes slightly red rimmed, the ears long and pendulous. Abundant folds of skin on the neck is one of the characteristics of the breed. The back slopes gradually towards the tail which is carried high when the dog is in action. The coat is short and close.

The colour is white with brown patches. Dogs stand 20–23in at the shoulder, bitches 19–21in.

Soviet Union

60 Gontjaja Estonskaja

This, one of the three Russian harrier/foxhound type varieties, is much less well known than the other two varieties, even in its country of origin: a dog show with an entry of two hundred gontjaja Ruskaja and over a hundred gontjaja Ruskaja pegaja would probably have only one or two of the Estonskaja variety. In type, however, it greatly resembles its cousins, although it appears to be slightly longer and lower cast. In colour it resembles the particolour or tricolour of the pegaja variety.

61 Gontjaja Ruskaja

The Russian canine world is still almost completely unknown to most people in the West. The only breeds with any claim to fame are probably the borzoi and the laika; the fact that there are special varieties of harrier/foxhound type is quite unknown.

Yet the more common Russian hound, the gontjaja Ruskaja, draws several hundred entries at the Russian hound shows in Moscow. It probably shares the ancestry of the European 'stövare' group, but in the course of time it has developed its own characteristics and is now considerably heavier and thicker set than most of its relations known to us. The head is cone shaped with a strong foreface and fairly long ears carried close to the head. The tail is long and thick, gradually tapering towards the tip. The coat is short and hard.

The colour is brownish black with lighter shadings. Height at shoulder is 22–24in.

Soviet Union

62 Gontjaja Ruskaja Pegaja

The particolour Russian hound has, with the exception of colour, very similar characteristics to the common gontjaja Ruskaja. The pegaja variety, however, generally seems to have shorter ears and tail. It is not as numerically strong as its self-coloured relative, but still draws large entries at dog shows in its native country. The body colour is white or cream with large tan patches, and either with or without a black saddle. Too much white is apparently not desirable. It is slightly taller than the gontjaja Ruskaja—often over 24in at the shoulder.

63 Grand Bleu de Gascogne

The grand bleu de Gascogne is one of the oldest hound breeds. It is descended from the ancient Phoenician harrier/foxhound types which in medieval times were crossed with bloodhounds. It is likely that it was established as a breed as early as the sixteenth century and it is believed to have been very popular—it was even used by the royal hunting parties and was highly praised for its good nose. As distinct from many other old French hunting breeds, the grand bleu de Gascogne has survived and prospered and even contributed to the formation of other new breeds like the petit bleu de Gascogne (246), basset bleu de Gascogne (245), etc.

The 'big blue' is a tall elegant dog with a long head and large pendulous ears. The chest is deep and the tail long, sometimes with a flag underneath. The coat, though not at all coarse, should not be too short and smooth.

The 'blue' colour is really a mass of small black markings on a white background, giving a merle impression. There are larger black patches on the head and sometimes on the body. Height at shoulder is 25–28in for dogs, 24–26in for bitches.

64 Greyhound *Great Britain*

In a way, the greyhound would be just as much a part of a future space age as it was in ancient times. Functional beauty does not age and few breeds have been given a conformation so suited to its purpose as the greyhound. Every detail indicates power and speed. At a trot, the action is smooth and supple, but the greyhound is at its best at full stretch—a good racing dog easily achieves a speed of 50mph on the straight.

Greyhound racing today is, of course, an artificial form of hunting and not the original purpose of the breed. Greyhounds have been used for coursing game for centuries, certainly from Roman times until the comparatively recent past. In Great Britain it was a favourite pastime of the landed gentry, whose feudal ancestors were so determined to keep the pastime exclusive to the upper classes that they prohibited their servants from owning a greyhound on pain of death. It remained the special favourite of the higher social orders until the upsurge in greyhound racing in the past few decades.

The greyhound is a classy, muscular and supple dog. All colours are acceptable in any shade from black to white, self-coloured or particoloured. Height at shoulder is between 28–30in for dogs, and between 27–28in for bitches. Weight is around 66lb.

Belgium

65 Griffon, Smooth
(Griffon Brabançon)

At the beginning of this century the rough-haired variety of the Belgian griffon (274) was crossed with, among others, the pug (13), which resulted in the smooth coat which now distinguishes the griffon Brabançon from the griffon Bruxellois (66). At first the smooth type was considered less desirable and was not used for breeding. But it was not long before a griffon with a smooth coat was regarded as just as attractive as a rough-haired one and soon the griffon Brabançon became recognised and respected as a breed in its own right, even though not seen as frequently as its rough-haired cousin. Inter-breeding between the two varieties is allowed and frequently practised.

With the exception of the coat, which in the griffon Brabançon is short and smooth, the two varieties are identical.

66 Griffon, Rough
(Griffon Bruxellois)

The griffon Bruxellois descends mainly from the now fairly rare breed of affenpinscher and from an ancient Belgian country breed of diffuse background. It did not take the rough griffon long to work its way up from farms and backyards to a position in society, and for a long time it was kept as a favourite at the Belgian Court. Of the two varieties of griffon, the Bruxellois is undoubtedly the one which has gained most appreciation internationally.

The griffon Bruxellois is a cobby, sturdy and lively dog with an alert and cheeky expression. The head is large with a short, wide muzzle and a slightly undershot mouth, without showing the teeth or tongue. The eyes are large and dark, the ears very small and semi-erect. The coat is rough and straight, forming an abundant beard on the chin.

The colour is either red, black or black and tan. White patches are highly undesirable. Weight varies considerably, but should preferably be under 10lb. The breed standard does not specify height.

France

67 Griffon Nivernais

The griffon Nivernais was originally used for wild boar hunting. The fact that such hunting is rarely practised nowadays may well be the reason for the breed's scarcity. With its rugged, unrefined looks it is unlikely ever to become a dog for the drawing room, but it is reputed to be very affectionate in the same slightly melancholic way as the bloodhound (18).

As a hunter, it was valued more for its strength, courage and stamina than for its speed. It is now a fairly .thick-set, heavy dog with rectangular body and mournful expression. The head is fairly small in relation to the body. The eyes are preferably dark and expressive, the ears pendulous. The tail is of moderate length and carried sabre-fashion, but may occasionally be slightly curled at the tip. The coat is profuse and coarse without curl.

The colour is preferably wolf grey or slate blue, but may also be black with or without tan markings, or even fawn. Height at shoulder is between 21–23in for dogs, proportionately less for bitches.

68 Griffon à Poil Dur *France*

In the nineteenth century, a man called Korthals worked at producing a special breed of gundog, an all-round dog which could be used for most purposes and would be a willing hunter of most game. He combined different continental gundog breeds, all specialists in their fields—mainly varieties of French water spaniel—and eventually arrived at what was then known as the Korthals griffon. It gained certain acclaim and was at one time very popular in Europe, but is now very rarely seen in its home country and hardly ever abroad, except in the USA.

This wire-haired griffon is a heavily built but not too long-legged dog. The head is long and narrow, the eyes large and amber or light brown. The ears are set high, carried dropped, of medium size and sparsely coated. The nose is always brown. The body and legs are strong and muscular and the tail docked to about one third of its length and carried in line with the back or slightly above it. The coat is rough and shaggy without curl which gives the dog an ungroomed look. There is also a long-haired variety, the griffon à poil laineux.

The colour is steel grey or light grey with chestnut-coloured patches. Height at shoulder for dogs is about 22in and about 20in for bitches.

France

69 Griffon Vendéen, Basset

There is something of both dachshund (191) and Dandie Dinmont terrier (204) about this very rare French breed, which
on no account conforms to what people in most countries
would describe as a basset breed.

There are two types: grand, illustrated here, and petit. The
smaller variety is of a much later date than the larger one
and, apart from size, the main difference is its considerably
shorter foreface. Both varieties, however, are rectangular in
build and have a rounded skull and a marked stop. The eyes
are large and dark with an affectionate expression. The ears
are long and pendulous. The tail is long and thick and carried
fairly high. The coat is profuse and coarse.

Both varieties of the basset griffon Vendéen may be self-
coloured, particoloured or tricolour in a variety of shades.
Height at shoulder for the grand basset griffon Vendéen is
15–17in, 13–15in for the smaller variety.

France

70 Griffon Vendéen, Grand

The griffon Vendéen is a French sporting dog which comes in at least four varieties. The largest of these, the grand griffon Vendéen, is likely to be the oldest. It was originally used for wolf hunting in its native country, but when the wolf died out the breed got a new purpose as it was found that it was faster than the griffon Nivernais for wild boar hunting.

The grand griffon Vendéen is extremely powerful and robust without being clumsy. The head is long, fairly narrow, but with powerful jaws. The eyes are always large, dark and keen, the ears soft, pendulous and fairly long. The tail is set relatively high and carried 'sabre-fashion but not as a scythe' as the breed standard states, somewhat obscurely. The coat is coarse and fairly long with particularly abundant moustaches and eyebrows.

The colour may be white with red, fawn or grey markings, fawn, 'hare-coloured' or tricolour. Height at shoulder is 24–26in.

71 Groenendael (Belgian Shepherd Dog)

An Alsatian? Not at all—even if to a layman it may look very similar. Undeniably, the Groenendael does resemble a black Alsatian (47) but there are many physical characteristics which separate the two breeds. Its more manageable temperament is one thing which ought to be enough to make this Belgian sheepdog just as popular as the Alsatian, at least as a pet and companion.

The Groenendael is one of the four different herding breeds which have guarded the herds in Belgium since ancient times. Not until the turn of the century was the classification introduced which made them into breeds in the modern sense (see also Tervueren, 226). The Belgian police force has used the Groenendael in its work for many years, but in other countries it is kept primarily as a companion.

It differs in appearance from the Alsatian mainly by its lighter and taller build. It has an alert and attentive expression, a pointed foreface, and eyes which vary in colour from amber to brown. The coat forms a mane round the neck and the tail is bushy. One peculiarity of the breed is that it prefers running in a circle rather than in a straight line.

The colour is black. Height at shoulder is 24–26in for dogs, 22–24in for bitches.

72 Greenland Dog
(Gronlandshund)

The Greenland dog belongs to the polar spitz breeds and is relatively rare outside its home country, where it is used as a sledge dog by the Eskimos. Generally, it leads a very independent life, is left to find its own food and is hardly ever kept indoors. It is, however, reputed to adjust easily to less rugged conditions further south and can become very affectionate.

In conformation, it is typical of the heavier and coarser spitz breeds—powerfully built with a bold, spirited expression. The head is proudly carried with a broad skull, small watchful slanting eyes, and rounded ears which, when the dog is alert, are very mobile. The dog is strong, with well boned legs and unusually large feet. The tail is short and tightly curled. The coat is very coarse, thick and straight, and is particularly close on the body, tail and in between the toes for protection against the cold. Any colour and mixture of colours is acceptable. Minimum height at shoulder for dogs is 24in, 22in for bitches.

Germany

73 Hanoverian Schweisshund
(Hannoveranischer Schweisshund)

The Hanoverian schweisshund has been bred specifically for the purpose of tracking wounded game. After various crosses at the beginning of the nineteenth century the type existing today was evolved, ideal for the task because of its sensitive nose and steady temperament.

The Hanoverian schweisshund is a sturdy, low-set dog with a quiet, tranquil disposition. The head is heavy and is usually carried low, with a slightly wrinkled forehead and very broad muzzle. The ears are long, without folds and carried close to the head.

The colour is greyish brown or red with darker markings on the muzzle, above the eyes and on the ears. White or light markings are not acceptable. Height at shoulder varies considerably between dogs and bitches: the dog may be up to 24in, while the bitch is normally about 18in.

Holland

74 Hollandse Herdershond, Smooth-haired
(Hollandse Herdershond, Kortharig)

The Hollandse herdershond could be described as the equivalent of the French berger varieties and the Belgian Groenendael (71) and Tervueren (226), and even the German Alsatian (47). But whereas in France and Belgium the varieties have been separated and given their own names, there is only *one* herding breed in Holland. Even though there are three varieties, since they differ from one another only in coat they are regarded as one breed. The smooth-haired variety is the most common while the long-haired is practically extinct; the wire-haired variety is considered less attractive by Dutch breeders. Very few examples of the breed have found their way outside Holland.

Accepted colours are fawn, red and brown; the smooth-haired variety is often cream or light and dark golden brindle, while the wire-haired herdershond may be greyish blue or pepper and salt. Height at shoulder may vary between 23–25in for dogs and about 1in less for bitches.

75 Hollandse Herdershond, Long-haired
(Hollandse Herdershond, Langharig)

Holland

76 Hollandse Herdershond, Wire-haired
(Hollandse Herdershond, Steilharig)

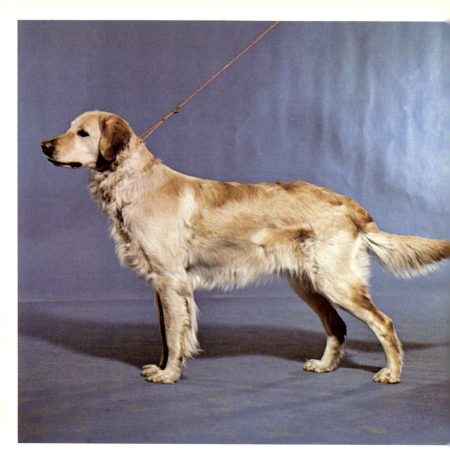

Germany

77 Hovawart

The hovawart evolved in southern Germany at the beginning
of this century and, although rarely seen outside its native
region, is a breed used both as a working/guard dog and
as a companion. The first part of its name comes from the
German word for farm, 'hof', the second part, 'wart', meaning
watch—thus a farm watchdog.

It is a fairly large breed and very active. The head is large
and rounded with drooping ears, the legs are straight and
the long tail has a flag. The coat is wavy with a soft undercoat.

The colour may be golden, black with brown markings
or possibly light brindle. Height at shoulder is 24–28in for
dogs, 22–26in for bitches.

Ireland

78 Irish Wolfhound

The wolfhound is an ancient breed, long used by the Irish Celts for hunting and often praised in Teutonic literature for its courageous qualities. When its traditional prey gradually disappeared from the island, there was no work for the wolf-hound and it was threatened with extinction. Only strenuous efforts by enthusiastic breeders saved it.

The Irish wolfhound is the largest breed in the world—a fully grown dog stands, on average, 32–34in at the shoulder. With its great size, impressive bulk and rough grey coat, it would seem that the wolfhound has everything needed to make it the ideal, awe-inspiring guard. Its threatening presence, however, is softened by its gentle, dark eyes and an affectionate, friendly disposition. As a companion and pet the wolfhound is docile and manageable and, partly because of these attributes, needs less space than one would imagine.

The Irish wolfhound is muscular and strongly, though gracefully, built. The coat is rough and especially long on the head. The colour is usually a shade of grey, but may be black, white, fawn, red or brindle. Minimum height for dogs is 31in, 28in for bitches.

79 Jämthund

The jämthund is regarded as a thoroughly Swedish breed. Although not officially recognised until 1946, predecessors of the jämthund have existed throughout northern Scandinavia for a very long time. The jämthund owes its existence as a breed to a few Swedish huntsmen who refused to accept the elkhound for their purposes and instead propagated the local jämthund type which, in their opinion, was better suited for elk hunting. It is now, numerically, one of the strongest breeds in Sweden, but is little known outside its home country.

The jämthund may be as much as 4in taller than the elkhound. It has a good reach and is agile, courageous and yet completely composed. The head is slightly longer than the elkhound's with a very strong, less pointed foreface. The ears are pointed and very mobile, the eyes dark with a keen expression. The tail, which has no plume, is carried fairly loosely and curled over the back. The coat is thick and close to the body but longer on the chest, neck, buttocks and tail.

The colour is grey with cream markings on the muzzle, cheeks, throat and under the body. Height at shoulder is 23–25in for dogs, 21–23in for bitches.

80 Japanese Spitz

The Pomeranian (128) has become so popular in the Japanese canine world that it has now helped to found this 'native' spitz breed in its new homeland. Exactly how the Japanese have managed this is not known, but the Japanese spitz is a less extreme copy of its British ancestor—not as short in body and with a slightly longer head and, above all, a more 'normal' size. The Japanese spitz may be likened to a samoyed in miniature as much as to a Pomeranian.

The specification of size and colour is unobtainable, but the Japanese spitz is usually light cream or white (most unusual in the Pomeranian). Height at shoulder is estimated to be a maximum of 12in.

Turkey

81 Anatolian Karabash Dog
(Karabash)

There is no doubt that the Anatolian karabash is an ancient breed closely related to the mastiff; even today it is used for its historic work of protecting grazing sheep against wolves. Outside Turkey it has remained virtually unknown, but a few dogs were recently exported to Britain. The breed is considered to have a very tough temperament, although it is rarely vicious.

The karabash is very powerfully built and its massive head and broad forehand give the impression of being heavier in front than in the hindquarters. The ears are v-shaped with the tips falling forwards. The eyes are golden brown and set well apart. The tail is long, curls into a ring at the end with a suggestion of a flag. It is carried low, except when the dog is on the move in which case it is raised in a wide arch over the back.

The colour varies from cream to fawn, but may also be brindle with a black mask and black ears. Weight is around 88–143lb; height at shoulder is 26–30in, the dog always being considerably taller than the bitch.

Finland

82 Karelian Bear Dog
(Karjalankarhukoira)

Strictly speaking, the Karelian bear dog belongs to the Russian spitz breed varieties, the laikas. Originally it did not exist west of the Finnish border but selective breeding, carried out chiefly in Finland in the 1930s, has led to the breed spreading throughout northern Scandinavia. One possible reason for this is that since its original prey, the bear, has become rarer it has proved itself to be well-suited for elk hunting. A sturdy disposition and a reserved but courageous temperament are the most characteristic qualities of the Karelian bear dog which, however, 'must not be dangerously aggressive towards people' according to the breed standard!

The head is typical of the spitz breeds with erect ears and dark, alert eyes. The tail is curled, preferably not bobbed or short. The coat is straight and coarse, hanging loosely away from the body.

The colour is black shading into brown, often with white markings on the head, neck, abdomen, legs and tip of the tail. Height at shoulder is 21–24in for dogs, 19–21in for bitches.

Holland
83 Keeshond

For centuries the Keeshond was used as a guard-dog by Dutch farmers and fishermen and as a barge-dog on the Dutch canals. It did not really emerge into the limelight until the 1920s when a British breeder took an interest in the breed.

The Dutch were aware of the Keeshond's qualities at the same time as it became very popular in Britain. Its name probably stems from Jan Kees, formerly a very common name among Dutchmen.

The Keeshond is short and compact with a bold expression. A unique feature of the breed are the so-called 'spectacles', ie lighter shadings round the dark, almond shaped eyes. The ears are small and erect, the body deep and sturdy and the tail tightly curled, even with a double curl, over the back. The coat is thick and straight, hanging loosely from the body, and is particularly abundant around the neck, where it forms a large ruff, and on the buttocks.

The colour is all grey with dark tips. Height at shoulder is about 18in for dogs, 17in for bitches.

84 Kelpie

The Australian sheepdog, the kelpie or 'barb' as it is some-times called, is thought to have emerged as a breed in about 1870. Despite its comparative modernity it has made itself indispensable as a sheepdog and fathered the smaller but tem-peramentally tougher, Australian cattle dog. The kelpie is considered to have exceptional qualities of scent, sight and hearing and plays a key role on Australia's vast sheep rearing stations.

The kelpie is a clean-cut, tough and muscular dog with a foxlike head and expression. The stop is well defined, the eyes almond-shaped and may be light or dark according to the colour of the coat. The ears are set wide apart and carried erect at a slight angle. The neck is clearly arched. The body is lithe, the back of moderate length giving a rectangular out-line. It is not too heavy in bone, the feet are well knuckled up with hard pads and strong nails. The tail is bushy and is carried low in repose or high in action. The coat is short, straight, thick and feels rough to the touch.

The colour may be black, black and tan, red, red and tan, fawn, chocolate or smoke blue. Dogs stand about 19in at the shoulder, bitches about 1in less.

Hungary

85 Komondor

You can't help noticing a komondor. With its vast, always ungroomed coat (which, by tradition, should not be interfered with) it attracts attention from layman and dog expert alike. It is a very old breed and is mentioned in medieval Hungarian literature. It is still used for herding cattle and sheep. The coat, which consists of either flat or round 'cords', protects it as effectively from the heat in summer as from the cold in winter. The komondor has also proved to be an excellent pet and has become quite popular as a show dog, notably in the USA.

The colour is always white. Minimum height at shoulder for dogs is 26in, 22in for bitches. Ideal heights are 32in and 28in respectively.

86 Kromfohrländer

This breed, still very rare, is really a hunting dog and was not recognised in its home country, Germany, until twenty years ago. It is reportedly used even today as a hunting terrier in some parts of Europe. It originates from crosses between wire-haired fox terriers and a griffon breed from Brittany.

The kromfohrländer has a flat, wedge shaped skull, hardly any stop and a powerful, fairly broad foreface. The ears are set high and v-shaped. The back is straight and broad with a deep chest. The tail is set high and carried curled to the left side of the back. The coat is short but coarse.

The colour is white with brown patches. Height at shoulder is 15–18in.

87 Kuvasz *Hungary*

The kuvasz is a very old Hungarian breed, whose name is said to stem from a Turkish word for the 'guardian of the peace'. The breed serves as a guard nowadays, although earlier it was used to some extent for hunting larger game. As a pet and companion it is reported to be friendly, affectionate and intelligent but, above all, very watchful. Even though it is sometimes seen at dog shows in the USA, it has not spread outside its home country very much. Possibly it has been held back by its vague resemblance to the even more imposing Pyrenean mountain dog.

A typical kuvasz is tall and powerful with slow, dignified movement. The shape of the head is very important: it is noble and expressive and the foreface is neither sharp nor coarse. The eyes are dark brown with a fierce expression. The tail is carried low except when the dog is alert in which case it may be slightly raised; the tip of the tail is often hooked. The coat is short on the head, ears and feet, but long, wavy and fairly coarse, especially around the neck, on the tail and on the back of the legs (see also Slovakian kuvasz 164).

The colour is pure white, but ivory shades are acceptable. Height at shoulder is 28–30in for dogs, 26–27in for bitches.

88 Laika, Karelian

The Karelian laika, or Russian-Finnish laika, greatly resembles the Finnish spitz (187) and is considerably smaller than other varieties of laika. The laikas are used as barking gundogs (dogs used to attract the huntsman's attention to birds, by continual barking. Its name comes from a word for 'barking'.) The laikas are also used for sledge hauling and even cattle herding. In hunting they are used to pursue a variety of small game including ermine, squirrel and wild cat—they are truly all-round workers.

The Karelian laika variety is generally found near the Finnish border, but is nowadays not very common even there. It is of square build with a leaner, more pointed head than the Russian-European laika and has a tightly curled tail. The coat is thick and close.

The colour is a yellow-fawn in various shades, and height at shoulder between 16–19in.

89 Laika, Russian-European

The laika sprang to fame in the West some ten years ago as the 'space dog'. The dog used by the Russians in their space experiments was undoubtedly of laika type and the name of the breed was soon known the world over. It is not perhaps so widely known that the laika comprises a group of several breeds or that these breeds are primarily used as barking gundogs in their home country.

The Russian-European laika is the medium-sized representative of the laika family. It is sturdily built with dark, slightly obliquely set eyes, a thick rough coat and a curled tail.

The colour is grey, fawn or black and reddish grey. Height at shoulder varies from about 20in to 25in.

Soviet Union

90 Laika, West-Siberian

The West Siberian laika is only one of five different varieties of laika spread throughout the northern parts of the Soviet Union. None of the varieties has become very common outside their home areas where they are used as combined farm/guard/hunting dogs.

Its greatest claim to fame is probably as the 'space dog' and it is reportedly much used for medical experimental purposes in the Soviet Union.

Like most spitz breeds, the West Siberian laika is a lively and energetic dog. It is robust with a fairly long body, a wedge shaped head with ears of triangular shape and obliquely set eyes.

It is of medium size and often white in colour with orange patches. Colour, however, as well as height at shoulder may vary considerably.

91 Laplandic Herder

(Lapinporokoira)

When communications between the native peoples of Lapland in northern Scandinavia increased a few decades ago, their dogs interbred with various southern breeds. This led to a curious situation in which the southern breeders preserved the pure strain of the original Lapphund while the Laplanders' own dogs were virtually ruined for their job of herding reindeer by crosses with wholly unsuitable dogs like hounds and other hunting breeds. The Laplanders subsequently set about breeding out these imported undesirable traits and the result became known in Finland as the Laplandic herder. (In Sweden, a similar variety not yet officially recognised as a breed is called the 'reindeer herder').

In looks, the Laplandic herder is very similar to the Lapphund (92): the breed standard does not mention any significant differences, except that the Laplandic herder stands 19–22in at the shoulder for dogs, 17–19in for bitches. It may also carry its tail dropped.

92 Lapphund

The Lapphund's traditional role has been to assist his Lap-lander master in herding reindeer. Originally the dog may have been used for hunting wild reindeer, but when the Lap-landers domesticated their reindeer the Lapphund was retrained to become an outstanding herder. When the Lap-landers found other livelihoods, apart from reindeer rearing, the situation became critical for the Lapphund. It was saved, however, by a sudden interest in the breed in the southern parts of the country and is now well on its way to becoming popular as a pet and companion.

The dogs remaining in Lapland are often the result of crosses with other breeds. Those specimens, however, which were 'exported' to the south at an early stage have generally remained of pure breeding.

The Lapphund is a fairly low-set dog, a little under medium size, but is in all respects a typical spitz. The coat is profuse and almost lank.

The most desirable colour is considered to be dark brown, but black is most common. Brown and white, however, are also acceptable. Height at shoulder for dogs is 18–20in, 16–18in for bitches.

93 Leonberger

The Leonberger is a German breed which has appeared during the last century through crosses between St Bernard, black and white Newfoundland (the so-called Landseer variety) (105) and Pyrenean mountain dog (34)—a highly international mixture. It is still very unusual in most countries.

The head is broad with a domed skull and a marked stop. The ears are highly set but rather big, soft and pendulous. The coat is thick, fairly long and hangs slightly away from the body.

The colour is fawn, grey-fawn or orange, generally with darker markings around the muzzle and eyes. Minimum height at shoulder for dogs is 30in, 28in for bitches.

94 Lhasa Apso

The Lhasa apso is a Tibetan toy breed which is now frequently found a long way from its country of origin. It is still fairly rare in some countries, however, and is often mistaken—at least in Europe—for the more common shih tzu (161).

In the main, the two breeds have a common ancestry, but the Lhasa apso is generally regarded as having remained pure and without interbreeding with the Chinese toy dogs, which were occasionally sent as gifts to prominent Tibetans. The name of the breed stems from the Tibetan word for goat—because of its supposed likeness to the long-haired Tibetan goats. In looks, the Lhasa apso differs from the shih tzu mainly in its moderately larger size, heavier build and slightly longer foreface.

The most common colour is golden, which is fairly rare in the shih tzu. Height at shoulder is 9–10in for dogs, slightly less for bitches. The weight is around 8–15lb.

Norway

95 Lundehund

The lundehund is unique in the canine world, not only because of its five fully developed toes on each foot but also because it has for centuries lived completely isolated from other breeds on the small islands of Vaeröy and Röst off the coast of northern Norway.

The breed is still rare, even in Norway, and hardly known at all outside Scandinavia. It takes its name from the 'lunde' bird (the puffin), which it used to hunt, creeping into the bird's rocky nests under cover of darkness in order to kill its prey and carry it to the waiting huntsman.

The lundehund is a small lively spitz, but lacks the clean-cut reach characterising other spitz breeds. It has a slightly hook-shaped snout, the ears are erect, pointing forward and peculiarly supple. The feet have unusually large pads and each leg has double dewclaws (the dewclaw is the extra, undeveloped toe just above the foot on the inside of the leg which is often removed on newly born puppies). The coat is close, abundant and sleek.

The colour is grey, black or brown in varying shades and with white markings. Height at shoulder is 14–15in for dogs, 13–14in for bitches. Weight is around 13lb.

96 Lucerne Laufhund
(Luzerner Laufhund)

The Lucerne laufhund differs from other harrier/foxhound type breeds by its light build, giving the impression of an elegant, rather refined dog. Like its close relative, the Swiss laufhund (150), the Lucerne laufhund has been fairly extensively exported in recent years, but has as yet not reached the former dog's popularity abroad.

The head is long and narrow with a domed skull and dark eyes. The ears are set low and well back and are very long, thin and supple. The legs are comparatively long and fine in bone, the feet are small and the tail is carried in an upward arch in action. Its elegance and reach make it look fairly rangy. The coat is smooth and glossy. The colour is a mottled grey or black with large dark patches on the body and skull and tan markings on the head, body and legs. Height at shoulder is at least 16in.

97 Magyar Agár

The Magyar agár, a Hungarian sighthound, has in common with other sighthound breeds, a long history: sighthounds are depicted on Hungarian tombstones of the ninth century. The breed obviously shares its ancestry with other sighthounds, but was kept from interbreeding with them for a thousand years. Not until the nineteenth century was blood introduced from the British greyhound (64). The Magyar agár still differs in type from the greyhound: it is less strikingly elegant and is more of an all-round coursing hound.

The Magyar agár is muscular, strongly built, with a well defined body. The head has a less pronounced stop than that of the greyhound, the ears do not have the same lift, even when the dog is alert, and the tail usually curls into a ring at the end. The coat is short and smooth, but often grows longer during the winter.

The colour varies but is usually black or brindle, sometimes particoloured. The breed standard does not specify height, but weight should be about 59–68lb for dogs, 48–57lb for bitches.

Belgium
98 Malinois

The main difference between the Belgian malinois and its two relatives, the Tervueren (226) and the Groenendael (71) is the coat and, in the latter case, the colour. The malinois is of the same type as its relatives—it can be likened to a lighter, leggier Alsatian—and was used as a sheepdog to about the same extent in its home country. It is, however, much more like the Alsatian in coat texture than its more long-coated relatives. It is interesting that all three varieties of Belgian sheepdog have the same marked aversion to moving in a straight line and instead tend to move in circles.

The malinois and the Tervueren are the same colour: the coat varies from fawn to mahogany with black tips, slightly lighter on the dog's underside. White is only acceptable on the toes, as is a small white spot on the chest. Height at shoulder is 24–26in for dogs, 22–24in for bitches.

Italy

99 Maltese (Maltezer)

The small white, very charming Maltese is the oldest toy breed in the West. It does not originate from Malta, as one would think, but from another Mediterranean island with a similar name, Melita, where it has been found depicted on relics dating back to 900BC.

The Maltese has been a popular pet among the nobility for centuries, and even though it has changed a little over the years it is still largely the same breed that it was in ancient times.

Underneath its flowing coat, the Maltese is of distinct terrier type, albeit with a rather low-set body. The jet black nose peeps out from under the coat, while the eyes may be hidden by luxuriant hair. The coat is the breed's most prominent feature: it is very long all over, straight and silky.

Pure white is the most desirable colour, but all colours are acceptable—according to the Italian breed standard—as long as the dog is not particoloured (slight lemon markings on a white dog are acceptable). In common with most toy breeds, the Maltese should be as small as possible. Weight should not exceed 8lb and height at shoulder should not be above 10in.

100 Spanish Mastiff
(Mastin Español)

The Spanish mastiff also goes under the names of mastin de Estremadura or mastin de la Mancha in its home country, but they are all one and the same breed. Like most of its near relatives it was at one time used in battle, later for arranged dog fights. Nowadays it is used for wild boar hunting as well as guarding sheep or cattle. The custom of cropping its ears and docking its tail was inherited from its fighting days but the practice is now frowned upon and the breed is generally left in its natural state.

It is a powerful, heavily built and imposing dog, yet not so heavy that it appears inactive and clumsy. The head is broad with a rounded skull, well defined stop and small ears dropping forward to the cheek. The tail is thick and fairly short, carried low in repose and slightly curved in action. The hind legs also have dewclaws.

There are several colour varieties: most common are wolf grey, fawn, brindle, or white with black, fawn or grey markings. Weight is usually around 110–132lb. Height at shoulder is 26–28in, dogs always standing considerably taller than bitches.

101 Neapolitan Mastiff
(Mastino Napoletano)

Italy's own impressive version of the mastiff did not make much impact on the modern canine world until the mid-1940s. However, there is plenty of evidence, some of it geographical, that it may be a descendant of the battle dogs of Ancient Rome. Today, it is used as an imposing guard dog by the Army and the police but in the home it is reputed to be very docile and friendly.

The Neapolitan mastiff is one of the largest and heaviest breeds. It has an enormous and massive head with plenty of loose skin. Its ears are always cropped short in its native country. The colour of the eyes should match, or be darker than, the coat colour. The tail is sabre-shaped and is not carried over the back.

Acceptable colours are black, grey and brindle—occasionally with small white spots on the chest and toes. Height at shoulder may be up to 30in, but averages between 26–28in for dogs and 24–27in for bitches. Weight varies between 110–154lb.

102 Mastiff

The type represented by the big, heavy mastiffs is very ancient. The Babylonians prized it and it was frequently used by the Romans in their savage circus games. The forerunner of the mastiff has existed in Britain at least since Caesar's time and been used for a variety of purposes, though mainly to guard private dwellings.

In modern times, St Bernard (143) blood has been introduced in attempts to produce a mastiff 'as big as a bull'—reputedly the size of mastiffs in the distant past. Today, the mastiff is fairly rare even in Britain and is hardly ever seen in other countries.

The mastiff is a tall, powerful dog considerably larger than its relative, the bullmastiff (29), but not as heavily built. Its nose is not as blunt, but still broad and square. The eyes are small and should be as dark as possible. It has a greater reach of neck than the bullmastiff and is considerably higher in the leg. The tail is fairly long, but never carried above the level of the back. The coat is short and close.

The colour is usually fawn with black on the muzzle and ears and around the eyes. Dogs stand about 30in at the shoulder, bitches about 28in.

103 Mudi

The Hungarian herding breed, the mudi, differs considerably from the Hungarian 'coated' breeds of komondor and puli—sheepdogs which have attracted much more interest internationally. The mudi, which is closer to the sheep and cattle dogs of the West, emerged as a breed towards the end of the last century and is apparently a pure product of its own country. Despite its size, it is commonly used for herding cattle and has, as one would expect, an extremely bold and lively temperament. In recent years it has proved to be an excellent guard dog and an untiring ratter.

The mudi is slightly longer than its height at the shoulder. It has a long head with a pointed muzzle and hardly any stop. The ears are v-shaped, pointed and erect, the eyes oval, dark and slightly obliquely set. The tail is short (either by nature or through docking, since the breed standard stipulates a length of 'two or three fingers'). It is usually carried hanging down.

The colour is either black or white, occasionally a combination of the two, in small even spots. Height at shoulder is 14–19in.

Germany

104 Small Münsterländer
(Kleiner Münsterländer)

In looks, the small Münsterländer can be described as something between a cocker spaniel (170) and a setter (156–158), but the breed is not the result of any modern cross-breeding; it has existed in Germany for several centuries. Like the Brittany spaniel (54), it is used both as a retriever and as a pointing gundog—the role, in fact, of the setter and the pointer. Although recognised as a breed since the beginning of this century, it is not commonly found outside Germany.

The small Münsterländer also resembles the Brittany spaniel, but is slightly smaller and has a long tail.

The colour is usually liver roan and white with larger liver-coloured patches. Height at shoulder is 20–22in for dogs, 19–21in for bitches.

105 Newfoundland

Today, the large, reassuring Newfoundland is very popular as a pet and its robust build in combination with its tranquil temperament makes it an ideal companion for children. Its origin is largely unknown, but the breed owes its present standing to the British. The ancestry of the Canadian dogs which became resident in Britain in the eighteenth and nineteenth centuries is not known and for a long time breed type was very mixed.

Thanks to the famous painter of landscapes and animals, Edward Landseer, who became interested in the breed and often painted it, the dogs from Newfoundland quickly became very popular. Planned breeding resulted in the more even type which we see today.

At one time particoloured dogs were considered preferable (this variety was called after Landseer and still carries his name), but these were soon outclassed by the self-coloured blacks. Average height at shoulder is 28in for dogs, 26in for bitches, with an average weight of 145lb and 115lb respectively.

106 Norrbotten Spitz
(Norrbottenspets)

Although it was almost extinct for some years, the norrbotten spitz came to life again in the 1960s and has thus become one of the most controversial Scandinavian spitz breeds. It is, in fact, an ancient breed which has long been used in the northern parts of Sweden as a barking gundog as well as a guard and even herding dog. Its origin is obscure, but it would not be far wrong to regard it as the Swedish equivalent of the Finnish spitz and the Norwegian buhund.

For many years its appearances at official canine events were not very frequent and in 1948 the breed was labelled 'extinct' and removed from the register of the Swedish Kennel Club. A few years ago, isolated examples were found which resembled the old type. Interest was rekindled and before long sufficient breeding stock was available for breeding to be resumed and the norrbotten spitz was restored to the Kennel Club register.

The norrbotten spitz is small, lively and alert. The basic colour is preferably white with black, fawn or red markings. Height at shoulder is about 16in.

107 Norwegian Buhund
(Norsk Buhund)

As distinct from its relative, the elkhound (108), the Norwegian buhund has not been used for hunting; its traditional role is that of a farm dog and an outstanding one at that. Usually the elkhound and the buhund lived side by side on the Norwegian farms, each one utilised for his own particular purpose.

In common with many other spitz breeds, the buhund has proved to be an excellent herder and is still occasionally used as a sheepdog. It takes its name from the Norwegian word for farm. Unlike most other Scandinavian spitz breeds, the Norwegian buhund has evoked considerable interest abroad, notably in Britain.

The buhund is a lively and bold spitz of medium size. The head is light and wedge shaped, the eyes dark, alert and expressive, the ears pointed and mobile. The neck is of good reach, the body short and taut. The tail is fairly short and thick and curled over the back.

The colour is fawn or light red, grey fawn or black, preferably but not necessarily without white markings. Dogs stand about 18in at the shoulder, bitches slightly less.

108 Elkhound (Norsk Elghund, Grå)

Despite its long history, the elkhound is in many respects a manufactured breed. At the turn of this century the Scandinavian kennel clubs appointed a committee to establish the relationship between the various local varieties of spitz and to determine how the Scandinavian elkhound should look. As a result of these deliberations a dog very much resembling today's elkhound was chosen as the type to aim at. Thereafter, most breeders concentrated on this accepted type of elkhound and other local varieties fell into oblivion. As early as 1877, however, the elkhound was accorded a Norwegian breed standard and has since then remained the national breed.

The elkhound is an alert, bold dog with great energy—the sort of animal, in fact, that one would expect to find hunting elk. The head is wedge shaped, the eyes dark, the ears pointed and mobile. The tail is fairly short and tightly curled over the back. The coat is thick and profuse, longest on the buttocks, at the back of the forelegs, around the neck and on the tail.

The colour is varying shades of grey, lighter under the body. Height at shoulder is about 20in for dogs and about 19in for bitches.

109 Black Elkhound
(Norsk Elghund, Sort)

The black elkhound is fairly rare even in its homeland and practically unknown outside the Scandinavian countries. It evolved in the border country between Norway and Sweden and is relatively old as a pure spitz breed, having gained official recognition as early as 1877. In temperament it is considered less affectionate and considerably 'harder' than the elkhound with which, despite similar conformation, purpose and home country, it shares very little ancestry.

The black elkhound greatly resembles the elkhound but its coat is considerably shorter, which makes it appear lighter and larger.

The colour is always pure black and height at shoulder for dogs is 18–20in, slightly less for bitches.

Poland

110 Ogar Polski

The Polish hound, the ogar Polski, has remained almost completely unknown outside its country of origin. It has been bred over a long period of years for one particular purpose in a specific terrain. It is reputed to have a very sonorous voice.

The ogar Polski is considerably heavier in build than other mid-European and Scandinavian harrier/foxhound type breeds. The head is powerful with dark, slightly obliquely set eyes and fairly low-set ears carried close to the head. The tail is long and thick and, in action, carried in line with the back.

The colour is black, dark grey or dark brown on the body, with other parts in a slightly lighter shade of brown. Height at shoulder is 22–26in for dogs, 22–24in for bitches.

111 Old English Sheepdog

It is difficult to believe that the Old English sheepdog really is a cattle dog—that is, judging by a heavily coated show dog of today. Originally the aim was for a dog as big and as aggressive as possible in order to equip it to keep beasts of prey away from the herd. Since the breed has now become a pet and companion it has, in common with most other 'reschooled' breeds, become docile, friendly and affectionate. Its nickname, the bobtail—frequently an unofficial name for the breed—comes from the fact that its tail is docked very short.

The Old English sheepdog is a quaint-looking, heavily built dog with an abundance of coat all over. It stands slightly higher at the loins than at the shoulder and this gives it the characteristic rolling gait. The coat is not only profuse but shaggy and of good, strong texture.

The colour is usually greyish blue, with or without white markings. Height at shoulder for dogs is about 24in; bitches are slightly smaller.

112 Otterhound

One would not immediately connect the shaggy otterhound with the bloodhound (18), but underneath the coat their con-formation is very similar; the otterhound is also a near equal to the bloodhound in scenting powers. Although never seen at British dog shows, it is occasionally exhibited in the USA. Those who draw rash conclusions regarding its ancestry may be forgiven—at a first glance, the otterhound does undeniably look like a typical mongrel!

Underneath the coat, however, is a firm, muscular and sym-metrical body. The head is slightly broader than the extremely narrow and deep head of the bloodhound. The ears are long, thin and pendulous, giving the impression of nearly disap-pearing into the coat. The neck is moderately short and looks practically non-existent because of the abundant ruff around the neck. The tail is carried upwards but not curled and, like the rest of the dog, is covered with a hard and oily coat. The coat, incidentally, should not be soft and woolly.

The colour is usually a sandy fawn or a shaded grey with more or less diffuse black and tan markings. Height at shoulder is about 25in.

113 Owcharka

The Russian sheepdog breeds are grouped under the name owcharka; there are at least four different local varieties. They all descend from the spitz breeds, but have since been crossed with other breeds depending on local requirements for a suitable herder. In the Caucasus, for example, a really powerful owcharka was needed and the original type was crossed with the mastifff so that the dog would be able to defend the herd against wolves. This particular cross also had the advantage of retaining the thick, warm coat, essential in the hard Russian climate. Other varieties of owcharka are slightly smaller, usually not as heavily built and, with the exception of the long-coated variety in the south of Russia, not as profusely coated as the Caucasian owcharka. The latter is reputed to be very difficult to handle.

The colour varies a great deal: the Caucasian owcharka, illustrated here, is usually grey fawn but may also be white or even particoloured. Height at shoulder is about 26in.

Poland

114 Owczarek Podhalanski

This old Polish herding breed originated in the Orient, but
has settled down very well in its new environment. The larger
of the two varieties comes from the region of the Tatry mountains and is regarded as an excellent herder and courageous
and strong enough to defend the flock against intruders. It
is gentle and loyal to its master—positively dangerous to an
enemy!

The owczarek podhalanski is of roughly rectangular build
with dark eyes and an intelligent lively expression. The ears
are as wide at the base as they are long. The tail is long
with a slight curve at the end. The feet are large and oval
with very strong, hard pads. The coat is short and close on
the head and foreface, but longer and very thick on other
parts of the body, especially on the neck and rib cage. The
coat is straight or slightly wavy.

The colour is usually all white, sometimes a pale cream.
Minimum height at shoulder for dogs is 26in, 24in for bitches.

Poland

115 Owczarek Polski Nizinny

This, the smaller of the two Polish herding breeds, bears great resemblance to the Old English sheepdog (111) and the Tibetan terrier (222); if a common ancestry exists it is probably very distant, at least in the case of the latter breed. As mentioned already, the Old English sheepdog also belongs to the pastoral breeds.

According to the unusually enthusiastic breed standard, the owczarek Polski nizinny is a muscular dog with a profuse coat, intelligence and an exceptional memory. It is also easy to train and equally suitable as a pet in urban areas or as a sheepdog in the country.

Its length of back exceeds its height at the shoulder and the head looks disproportionately large because of the profuse coat. The ears are dropped, small and heart-shaped and the eyes are dark. The tail is either short by nature or docked. The coat, which is abundant and long all over, may be straight or slightly wavy.

All colours and combinations of colours are acceptable. Height at shoulder for dogs varies between 17–21in, while bitches stand 16–18in.

116 Papillon

Papillon is the French word for butterfly, and the breed could not have been more appropriately named. The ears are large with rounded tips and are set far apart and carried obliquely like the spread wings of the butterfly. Symmetrical markings on the head are also desirable, particularly an even white blaze which then forms the 'body' of the butterfly.

The type evolved between the 1550s and the period of the French Revolution, when it was a special pet of ladies-in-waiting and concubines at the French Court. The fall of the royal family also saw the fall of the royal dog and since then it has made its home in exile; the quality of papillons now bred in Belgium and Britain is as high as in its home country.

The papillon is dainty and elegant. The coat is long and silky forming profuse frills on the neck, chest and thighs. The ears are heavily fringed. The colour is white with black and/or red markings. Weight is around 4lb and height at shoulder should not exceed 12in.

117 Maremma (Italian Sheepdog)
(Pastore Maremmano-Abruzzese (Maremma))

The maremma is still extensively used as a sheepdog in its native country, Italy, but in addition has gained recognition as a pleasing pet and a magnificent show dog.

The extremely detailed Italian breed standard particularly emphasises its square build, the impressive head with its fairly small, v-shaped and dropped ears, the black nose and the dark eyes. Most important, however, is the coat which is white, long, slightly wavy and particularly abundant around the neck, on the buttocks and underneath the tail, which is carried low. The undercoat is thick and weather-resistant.

Small beige markings are acceptable on the white coat. Height at shoulder is 26–29in for dogs, 24–27in for bitches.

118 Pekingese

The Pekingese and its imperial past is often well known to people who have never heard of other, even more common breeds. For thousands of years, the Chinese kept dogs to exorcise evil spirits and these were bred to look as cruel and forbidding as possible. The dogs were held in high esteem and when miniatures appeared they were treated with great respect and considered so valuable that only the Emperor was allowed to keep them. More than any other breed, the Pekingese has had to adapt itself drastically in coming to terms with the more humble conditions in which it finds itself in the West. The 'Peke' has done so graciously, without losing a scrap of the infinitely superior air it has inherited from its imperial past!

The Pekingese is small, bold and a great individualist. The head is broad with large, lustrous eyes and a flat profile. The forequarters are thick-set and heavily boned with slightly bowed front legs, while the hindquarters are lighter and straight. The tail has a magnificent plume and is curved over the back. The coat is also particularly profuse on the neck, chest, thighs and at the back of the front legs.

All colours except liver are acceptable. Height at shoulder is 6–10in and weight 7–11lb for dogs, 8–12lb for bitches. Particularly small animals—so-called 'sleeve dogs' because they were carried in the wide sleeves of the Chinese—still appear in litters of puppies of otherwise normal size.

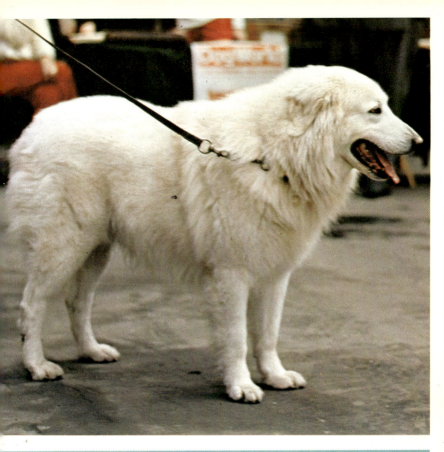

Spain

119 Perdiguero de Burgos

The Spanish pointer, the perdiguero de Burgos, has been prized as a gundog in Spain for centuries. It is rare outside its native country. As far as is known, it has remained a pure breed in recent years and its outstanding characteristic is stamina rather than speed.

The perdiguero de Burgos is neither as agile nor as elegant as the English pointer (127). It is not as square in body and has a long back, a large head with domed skull, a 'double chin' and high-set, long, pendulous ears. The tail is docked to one third of its natural length. The coat is smooth and short.

There are two colour varieties: when white is the basic colour, it should be marked with liver-coloured spots of varying sizes; on a liver-coloured dog the coat should be mottled with white. Height at shoulder for dogs is 26–30in, slightly less for bitches.

France

120 Phalène (Moth)
(Phalène)

The owner of a typical phalène gets told sometimes that his
dog would be a really fine papillon (116) were it not for its
ugly ears. In such circumstances the owner would be justified
in pointing out that the phalène was first on the scene. He
could add that the now typical 'butterfly' ears of the papillon
did not appear until after the French Revolution, when most
of the royal dogs lived in Belgium and were there crossed
with spitz breeds with erect ears!

The drop ears of the phalène are inherited from its spaniel
background, which it shares with the papillon. Unlike the
papillon, however, the phalène has not been subjected to
interbreeding.

With the exception of the ears, which should be completely
dropped, the breed is identical with the papillon. It is not
as popular, but now that it is recognised as a separate breed
it ought to stand a better chance of making its mark. Previously it competed in the same classes as the papillon at
dog shows.

Egypt

121 Pharaoh Hound

The Pharaoh hound represents one of the oldest types of dog. Opinions differ on whether sighthounds with erect ears evolved before the more common types with dropped ears. However, the frequently depicted god Anubis of the Ancient Egyptians bears a striking resemblance to the Pharaoh hound—which would thus be aptly named. It is not known when the Pharaoh hound's ancestors moved from Egypt to Malta, where it was rediscovered in modern times.

In conformation, the Pharaoh hound is noted for its clean-cut, graceful lines, its reach and proudly carried head with large, erect ears. The tail may be carried in action above the level of the back. The eyes are amber or dark brown and the coat short, glossy and smooth.

The basic colour is often white with patches of grey or red; predominantly red specimens are, however, most common and are preferred in Britain. Height at shoulder for dogs is 25–28in, 22–26in for bitches.

Italy

122 Italian Greyhound (Piccolo Levriero Italiano)

The Italian greyhound is the smallest of the sighthound breeds and is regarded as a toy dog in some countries. It is, however, a pure sighthound and was a popular pet for women in the days of the Roman Empire. It has not been subjected to interbreeding with other varieties.

As distinct from other sighthounds, the Italian greyhound has never been used for work to any serious extent, though as a favourite at the medieval European courts it was occasionally used for rabbiting—often together with falcons. Today, Italian greyhounds make good times on the race track in some countries.

In the show ring, great emphasis is placed on its elegance, fine bone and high-stepping, graceful action. It is well proportioned and sound, without appearing dwarfish. In many respects, it resembles its larger cousins the whippet (236) and the greyhound (64), but it is not only smaller but more slender in all respects.

Desirable colour and markings vary slightly from country to country; fawn, cream or blue, however, are always acceptable. Size and weight, too, vary between countries. Generally a weight not exceeding 10lb and height at shoulder of between 13–15in are considered the most desirable.

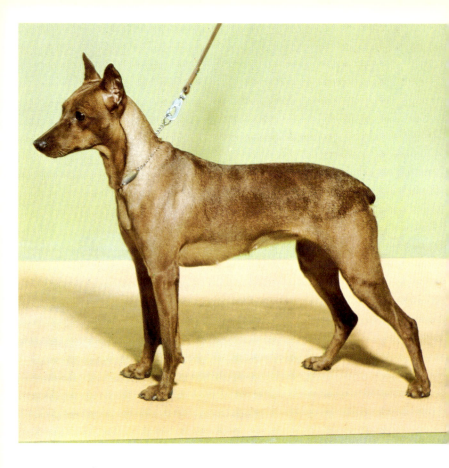

123 Pinscher

For some reason, the 'middle' pinscher has remained much less well known generally than either the larger or the smaller varieties: the Dobermann (50) and the miniature pinscher (124).

The pinscher, previously known as the German pinscher, is a very old breed and with its medium size ought to have a far wider appeal than it has. In common with the other pinschers it was originally used for ratting, but is now kept as a very alert and lively pet and companion.

In conformation, it bears a closer resemblance to the Dobermann than to the miniature pinscher. It is clean-cut, elegant and agile. The head is wedge-shaped with a long fore-face, the eyes dark and sparkling. The ears are carried with the tips falling forward or, as in its home country, cropped. The tail is docked, the coat is smooth and glossy.

The colour, as in other pinschers, is usually black with small tan markings or self red. Height at shoulder is 16–19in.

124 Miniature Pinscher
(Zwergpinscher)

The miniature pinscher has been one of the most popular toy breeds in the world for a long time: it is small, elegant and very lively. It evolved during the latter part of the nineteenth century when in some pinscher litters the odd miniature specimen was born. These were usually put down as unlikely to survive and unsuitable for any practical purpose.

Gradually, however, it was discovered that not only were they extremely vigorous but also very alert and pleasant companions. Interest grew and after some intensive breeding, the miniature pinscher became both graceful and popular.

In conformation, the miniature pinscher should as far as possible be a Dobermann in miniature. Characteristics are elegance, suppleness and a fiery temperament. The head is narrow and wedge–shaped, the eyes piercing black and the ears either stiffly erect or dropped. It should have neat bone, straight legs and sound action. The tail is docked short and carried a little high. The coat is short and glossy.

The colour is self red or black with tan markings. Height at shoulder should not exceed 12in and weight is around 6–8lb.

125 Plotthound

The plotthound may be described as a cross between two other fairly rare American breeds—the American foxhound (237) and the black and tan coonhound (43). Perhaps the closest resemblance is to a tall, heavily built common foxhound (58). The plotthound is not officially recognised as a breed by the American Kennel Club.

It is a very imposing dog with poise and a piercing expression. The colour is characteristic of the foxhound: white with patches of black and brown. It is regarded as the latest addition to the six varieties of coonhound.

126 Ibizan Hound
(Podenco Ibicenco)

The Ibizan hound is one of the rarer sighthound breeds—although whether it should be included among the sighthounds at all is open to question. It has quite a lot of trailing hound blood in its veins and its way of working—relying as much on powers of scent as on sight—is not typical of the sighthound. In conformation, however, it is nearly all sighthound—its sweeping outline, long head and long legs much resemble the greyhound's. Only the often erect, large ears betray strange blood.

The breed is most common on the island of Ibiza off the Spanish east coast where, in addition to the more common smooth-haired variety, wire-haired and long-haired types also existed at one time. An unusual characteristic of the Ibizan hound is its ability to jump: when hunting, it is said to be able to spring more than 6ft into the air in order to see which way its prey has gone!

The Ibizan hound is white with red or fawn patches, or self–coloured in any of these colours. The eyes are amber and the nose liver-coloured. Height at shoulder for dogs is 24–26in, 22–25in for bitches.

127 Pointer

The pointer's clean-cut outline is not almost immediately associated with British tweed and game shooting, yet in origin it is much less British than, for example, the setters. The pointer descends from European short-coated gundogs which up to the eighteenth century were imported to Britain and subsequently crossed with, among others, foxhounds (58). Today in its home country, it is as popular as a show dog as it is in the shooting field.

The hallmarks of the pointer are its clean, taut lines combining power with grace. The occiput and the stop are well pronounced and the bridge of the nose slightly concave. The eyes should not be lighter than hazel brown, preferably darker. The ears are fairly large and lie close to the head. The neck is long and nobly arched, the back slopes away to well angulated hindquarters. The tail is thick at the root, growing gradually thinner to the point and is carried level with the back; when the dog is in action it lashes from side to side. The coat is short, close and shiny.

The colour is white with black, lemon or liver markings, or black, liver or lemon with or without white. Dogs stand about 24in at the shoulder, bitches slightly less.

128 Pomeranian

A Pomeranian of the right sort is as appealing a creature as you are ever likely to find: from the midst of the usually fox-red coat a roguish little face with dark, bright eyes peeps out. It originates from German spitz breeds which were exported to Britain a few centuries ago. These Pomeranian spitz never became very popular, but interest was greater in the miniature puppies which occasionally cropped up in otherwise 'normal' litters. Bigger coats, smaller sizes and a great variety of colours were gradually produced by planned breeding, and even though the breed has dropped back slightly in numbers, it has retained a faithful group of fanciers throughout the world.

The ideal Pomeranian is so heavily coated that it becomes almost ball-shaped. The coat stands off from the body and is particularly profuse around the neck, chest, hindquarters and tail, from where it extends nearly to the back of the head.

Self-coloured dogs are preferred. Orange is most common, but all colours are acceptable, even particolours. Weight is about 4–5lb, and height at shoulder should not exceed 11in.

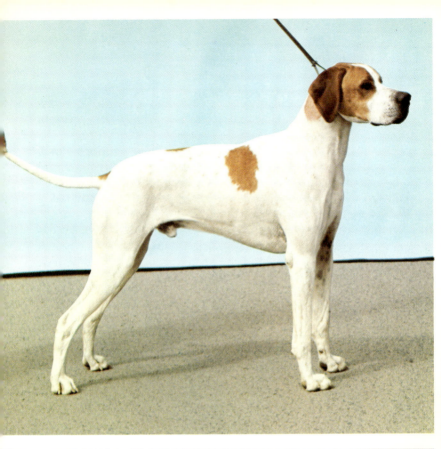

Germany

129 Poodle-Pointer

(Pudelpointer)

The name of the poodle-pointer makes one think of the 'home made' breeds of the bogus breeder, but even though the animal descends from both the poodle (31) and the pointer (127) you have only to look at a good example to realise that it really is a thoroughbred. It greatly resembles the German wirehaired pointer (48), is used for similar work and is just as versatile. It is, however, older as a breed.

The poodle-pointer has a noble bearing and graceful action, a broad head, powerful foreface and a pronounced stop. The ears are dropped and of medium size. The coat is coarse and particularly abundant around the eyes and on the chin, resulting in bushy eyebrows and whiskers.

The colour is brown or golden brown and height at shoulder varies between 21–26in.

Great Britain

130 Pug

For many years the pug has been regarded as the ultimate in spoilt lap dogs, a conception which is now giving way before the great charm of this highly original and delightful little dog. It looks as if the tide has turned, and few breeds deserve their popularity as much as the pug. With its friendly and cheerful temperament and its manageable size it is undeniably ideal for many people.

The pug came to Europe from Imperial China in medieval times and quickly became popular both in Holland and in Britain. It has changed very little over the years—except to become even sounder and more happily extrovert. Typical qualities of the breed are its compact, well-knit proportions, its jaunty movement and kindly disposition.

The colour is pure black or fawn with a black mask, black ears and a black trace along the back. Weight varies between 14–18lb and height at shoulder should not exceed 13in.

131 Puli

Not many Hungarian breeds have found their way out of their home country. The quaint little Hungarian puli is one of the few exceptions and is probably the one which has become most well known, though it is still a rarity in most countries. It has been, in turn, a hunter, a sheepdog and now a pet and companion. It was not seen abroad until the 1920s and outside its native country it is probably most popular in the USA.

The puli is an alert dog of medium size; its main characteristic being the profuse coat, which is long and wavy with a tendency to tangle. The head appears almost round on account of the plentiful hair, the eyes are slightly slanted with a bright expression and the ears are dropped. The tail is carried curled over the back.

The colour may be black, grey or white. Height at shoulder is 15–19in for dogs, 13–17in for bitches.

Hungary

132 Pumi

The Hungarian sheepdog, the pumi, descends from the better known puli which was crossed with sheepdogs from France and Germany in the eighteenth and nineteenth centuries. Originally it was used mainly as a sheepdog, but now it is used primarily as a guard dog and sometimes for hunting. It is unknown outside Hungary, where it is found mostly in the country. With its mongrel looks, it is unlikely ever to become an exclusive show dog!

The pumi is a lively little dog with a long, powerful foreface and semi-erect ears. The eyes are dark and slightly slanting. The tail is carried in line with the back, or slightly lower, and is docked to two thirds of its natural length. The coat is profuse, wavy but coarse.

Several colours are acceptable, but various shades of grey are most usual. Particoloured dogs are considered undesirable. Height at shoulder is 13–17in.

133 Redbone

The redbone is one of six varieties of coonhound which exist in different parts of the USA and is perhaps the best known of the five which are not officially recognised by the American Kennel Club. The sixth, and recognised, variety—the black and tan coonhound (43)—appears infrequently at American dog shows. The redbone is not only of different type, but is also considered a more efficient water dog than its officially recognised relative.

The black and tan coonhound is akin to the bloodhound (18) in looks and was therefore recognised as a separate breed; the other coonhound varieties were all considered to be too like the foxhound (58) to get recognition as separate breeds. The redbone therefore lacks any affinity with the bloodhound but, today, it cannot be described as identical with any of the foxhound varieties either. It is far lighter and leggier than the common foxhound (58).

The colour is always a glossy, leonine golden. Height at shoulder is about 26in.

134 Chesapeake Bay Retriever

The Chesapeake Bay retriever is *the* American water retriever. Its similarity to the British (that is, almost entirely 'made in Britain') Labrador retriever (138) may be striking to the layman—Labrador blood dominates its ancestry—but as distinct from most other related breeds, the Chesapeake Bay retriever has pure yellow eyes and a very special coat: slightly wavy on the back and very short, tough and thick on the body in order to withstand cold and wet when working in icy waters. The coat should feel decidedly oily to the touch and should be so water-resistant that once the dog has come ashore and given itself a shake, it should feel hardly damp! The colour is also considered very important: in order that the dog should merge with its background as far as possible, the breed standard lays down a 'deadgrass' colour for the coat, ie from a dark brown to a faded tan, preferably without small white markings on chest and feet. Dogs stand 23–26in at the shoulder, bitches 21–24in.

Great Britain

135 Curly-coated Retriever

The peculiar coat of the curly-coated retriever quickly distinguishes it from other retriever breeds and demonstrates its Irish water spaniel (173) and poodle ancestry (31). In addition to this lineage, it descends from largely the same type of Old English hunting spaniel and imported Canadian dogs as the golden and Labrador retrievers. As an established breed it is, however, one of the oldest within the group.

The curly-coated retriever is a strong, upstanding dog, in conformation as well as deportment. It is also intelligent and active with great stamina. The head is powerful with a moderately flat skull, the eyes are black or brown and rather large, but not too prominent. The ears are small, lying close to the head. The neck, body and legs are strong and muscular. The tail is moderately short and is carried fairly straight. The coat is the main characteristic of the breed: it is a mass of small, crisp curls all over, including the ears and tail but excluding the muzzle.

The colour is black or liver. Height at shoulder is about 25–27in.

136 Flat-coated Retriever

This still fairly uncommon gundog breed should have been called by another name, as originally its flat coat was by no means characteristic of the breed. Most dogs being shown when the breed was in its infancy had a decidedly wavy coat. This type of coat gave way to the appearance found today, after interbreeding with other breeds including setters and, possibly collies. The Labrador retriever is thought to have played the biggest part in the evolution of the flat-coat, which was regarded as a separate breed as early as in the 1850s.

The flat-coated retriever is powerful yet racy, without appearing either cumbersome or lanky. The eyes are hazel or dark brown with an intelligent expression and the ears are small and carried close to the side of the head. The coat is close, fine in texture and should be as flat as possible. Fore and hindquarters are well feathered.

The colour is black or liver. Height at shoulder is about 23in and weight about 65lb.

Great Britain

137 Golden Retriever

Although the golden retriever is a pure gundog its many good qualities have gradually made it as valued in the home as in the shooting field. In the last decade it has become increasingly popular as a pet because of its open, friendly temperament.

The beginning of the breed can be dated exactly as 1886, when a litter of golden-coloured puppies of mixed retriever/ spaniel ancestry was born on an estate in Scotland. The puppies proved to be excellent gundogs, the strain was largely kept pure and at the beginning of this century the golden retriever began to establish itself.

It is a well-porportioned dog, active, docile, powerful and yet stylish. The coat is either flat or wavy, close, water-resistant and with good feathering, especially on the tail.

The colour may be any shade of gold or cream, neither too dark nor too light. Dogs stand 22–24in at the shoulder, bitches 20–22in, while weight is about 67lb and 57lb respectively.

n

13   Retriever

Desp   abrador retriever is a British breed;
some   re Canadian dogs taken to Britain
aboar   in the case of the golden retriever,
Labra   ence to someone trying to produce
a goo   particular purposes, who bred a
few lit   essful that his dogs were sought
after al

It wa   as a breed by the Kennel Club
in 1903   ined great popularity, originally
as a wo   ow increasingly as a pet. The
general a   ador is that of a strongly-built,
powerful

The co   or yellow, though some are
liver and t   ye and have a liver-coloured
nose. Heigl   t 22in for dogs, 21–22in for
bitches.

139 Rhodesian Ridgeback *South Africa*

The Rhodesian ridgeback has been advertised as 'a man's dog', the implication being that it is not a breed for the elegant drawing-room. Be that as it may, the fact is that the ancestors of today's ridgeback were used for lion hunting in Africa and were originally both hard-bitten and vicious in temperament.

The breed's origins are unknown, but it is likely that it stems from crosses between dogs belonging to the natives and those of the white population. It is now regarded as the national breed of South Africa. It was not officially recognised as a breed in Europe until well into this century, and even though it is rare in many countries it is quite numerous at British and, naturally enough, South African dog shows.

The Rhodesian ridgeback is a muscular and active dog. Its main characteristic is that the hair on the back grows in the opposite direction to the rest of the coat, forming a ridge along the spine. The head is of moderate length and rather broad. The ridgeback has round, sparkling eyes and its ears are carried close to the head. The coat is short, thick and glossy.

The colour is light to red wheaten, sometimes with a small white spot on the chest. Height at shoulder for dogs is 25–27in, bitches 24–26in. Weight is around 75lb.

140 Rottweiler

To the layman, the Rottweiler may look like a coarser, heavier version of the Dobermann (50). The two two breeds have little in common, however, except for colour and, possibly, the working dog's temperament, though the Rottweiler, like most large breeds, is more docile and phlegmatic. The Rottweiler comes from a longer line than the Dobermann: it is one of the purer descendants of the Roman fighting dogs. Gradually it developed into a cattle dog, but was probably used just as much to protect the herders against bandits. In recent years it has become the outstanding guard dog and its qualities have long been recognised by the German police.

The Rottweiler's heavy build, with strong bone does not prevent it from being agile. The head is fairly broad and rounded, the foreface powerful and the ears small and triangular in shape. The neck and body display strength and power. The tail is docked short and is carried in line with the back. The coat is close and short, slightly longer on legs and tail.

The colour is usually black with clearly defined tan markings. Dogs stand 24–27in at the shoulder, bitches 22–25in.

Arabian peninsula

141 Saluki

The saluki is the oldest of the sighthound varieties and is unique in the canine world since for thousands of years it has remained pure and been kept from interbreeding. Representations of the saluki dating back to about 6000BC illustrate that many of the finer points required of show dogs today were evident in the breed even then.

Since ancient times the saluki has been the prized companion of the desert Bedouins, well adapted as it is for work as a hound in the dry, burning desert. The Mohammedans regard dogs as 'unclean', but make an exception for the highly valued saluki, which may even be permitted to share its owner's quarters. In the West, the saluki is kept almost exclusively as a pet.

The body is lithe and graceful, the head finely chiselled and proudly carried. The coat is smooth and silky with long feathering on the ears and on the long, low-carried tail. Colours and sizes vary a great deal; dogs stand 23–28in at the shoulder, while bitches are proportionally smaller.

There is also a smooth-coated variety of the saluki which completely lacks feathering on ears and tail, but is in all other respects the same.

The Arctic

142 Samoyed
(Samoyede)

The samoyed was introduced to the West considerably earlier than other Arctic spitz breeds. It was very popular in Britain as early as the beginning of this century and was subjected to intensive breed improvement.

The typical show samoyed is a truly handsome creature, often managing to combine a presence which evokes a vision of endless snowy plains with an air of elegance and poise appropriate to the drawing-room. It exudes serenity, power and self-confidence.

The head is powerful, the eyes almond-shaped and set well apart. The ears are erect and slightly rounded at the tips. The tail, not as tightly curled as in most other spitz breeds, is carried over the back when the dog is alert. The coat is very profuse, especially around the neck, on the tail and on the feet.

The colour is usually pure white but may be cream, or white and biscuit-coloured. Height at shoulder is about 21in.

143 St Bernard
(St Bernhardshund)

For centuries the St Bernard has been the massively reassuring symbol of last-minute rescue. There are many fantastic stories about its ability to find and dig out travellers buried in Alpine snow drifts, and escort them to a monastery refuge.

These stories are nearly always grossly exaggerated, but it is a fact that Swiss monks at the St Bernard pass made good use of their large, powerful dogs for finding strangers who got lost in blizzards. But the St Bernard remained only a legend outside the cloister walls until well into the nineteenth century. When the St Bernard became superfluous in the Alps, it found another purpose in life—as a pet which has become cherished in many homes throughout Europe. With its docile manners, the former mountain rescuer is fairly easy to keep, despite its size.

The St Bernard is large heavy with a massive head and kindly, dark, often red rimmed eyes. It may be either rough or smooth-haired.

The colour is usually white and orange. Height at shoulder for dogs is at least 28in, preferably more; bitches are slightly smaller.

144 St Bernard, Rough
(St Bernhardshund)

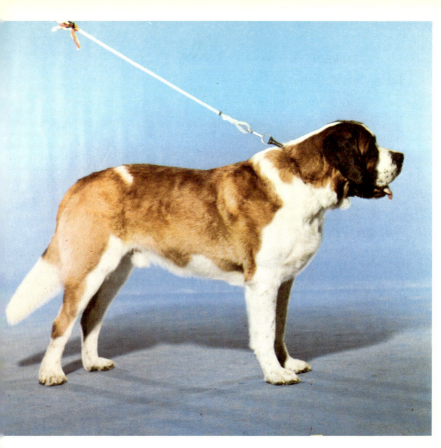

145 Sanshu

The sanshu is a medium-sized Japanese spitz breed which shares much of its ancestry with the chow chow; it also resembles a smooth chow in some ways. In Japan, the breed is used both as a guard dog and as a pet.

The sanshu is almost square in build with a broad, flat skull and dark almond-shaped eyes. The tail is curled over the back. The coat is not very long, but close and coarse to the touch.

Accepted colours are a rusty red, black and tan, tan, fawn, pepper and salt and particolour. Height at shoulder is about 20in—about 1in less for bitches, 1in or so more for dogs.

146 Schipperke

The little skipper, the schipperke, as its name suggests, evolved aboard Dutch canal barges. It was the British, however, who gave it its present stamp and made it popular. Originally, the type was very mixed and the schipperke could hardly be described as a breed, but after the British concentrated breeding among the smallest animals, breed type became even.

Thos developments took place less than a hundred years ago and since then, although the schipperke has gained considerably in popularity, it has not become particularly common. With its bright, foxlike expression and its manageable size it deserves to be better known.

The main characteristics of the breed are an intensively lively temperament, the foxlike head with a pointed foreface, and the stiffly erect ears. The eyes are small and dark brown, the body short and deep. The schipperke has no tail—puppies are occasionally born with a tail but this is an indication of poor blood somewhere in the bloodline. The coat is close and rough and forms a mane around the neck and good 'trousers' on the thighs.

The colour is usually black, but other whole colours are acceptable. Weight is around 12–16lb. Height at shoulder should not exceed 12in.

147 Standard Schnauzer
(Schnauzer)

In some countries, the two small varieties of schnauzer, the miniature and the standard, are classified as belonging to the terrier group. Certainly the schnauzer could be described as Germany's answer to the terrier breeds of Great Britain.

Its type can be traced back to medieval times, or even earlier, although the schnauzer was not mentioned in literature until the nineteenth century. It has subsequently become much more even in type and highly popular in countries far beyond Germany, notably in Britain and the USA.

The standard schnauzer is a clean-cut, muscular, square-built dog with noble bearing and alert temperament. The head is elongated but does not have the extreme leanness of many of the British terrier breeds; the eyes are dark and oval with an intelligent expression and the ears are v-shaped and drop forward to the temple. They can be cropped, as in the schnauzer's native country. The coat is tough and wiry, particularly abundant on the head where it forms prominent eyebrows, a stubby moustache and chin whiskers.

The colour is pure black or pepper and salt with a darker mask around the muzzle. Dogs stand about 19in at the shoulder, bitches 18 in.

148 Giant Schnauzer
(Riesenschnauzer)

The impressive, bearded giant schnauzer is, strictly speaking, not a schnauzer at all but a good example of man's ability to breed living creatures to his own specifications.

Even though today's giant schnauzer is an almost identical larger copy of the smaller varieties, it mainly descends from German sheepdogs and cattle dogs. The 'schnauzer looks' were introduced through interbreeding with the smaller schnauzer breeds. When the need for cattle dogs diminished, the future of the breed became critical until its qualities as a police dog were discovered. It is still used for work in this field, but is mainly kept as a reliable and appreciated guard of house and home.

The breed standard for the standard schnauzer (147) and the miniature schnauzer (149) also applies to the Giant schnauzer, apart from size requirements, of course. Dogs stand around 26–28in at the shoulder, bitches 24–26in. The giant schnauzer generally appears less clean-cut and terrier-like in outline than the smaller varieties and often lacks their length of head and neck. The usual colour is pure black, though pepper and salt is not uncommon.

149 Miniature Schnauzer
(Zwergschnauzer)

The high-spirited miniature schnauzer is an exact copy, small scale, of the standard schnauzer. It is now probably equally valued as a pet. The breed has, however, a slightly different line from that of the standard schnauzer and became established somewhat by accident. Attempts were made at the turn of this century to save some German toy breeds from degeneration (toys had long been regarded as ornaments for the divan and not designed to lead a normal healthy life). As part of the revitalising process some toys were crossed with the smallest standard schnauzers available and after some skilful breeding, the perfect schnauzer in miniature resulted.

The miniature schnauzer is, as stated, a smaller version of the standard schnauzer and free from any suggestion of 'toyishness'—it should be just as muscular, vigorous and alert. In common with the standard schnauzer, its ears are cropped in some countries. The colour, too, conforms to the other varieties and should be either pure black or pepper and salt. Height at shoulder should not exceed 14in.

Switzerland

150 Swiss Laufhund
(Schweizer Laufhund)

Exports of harrier/foxhound type breeds from Europe to the rest of the world have increased in recent years. One of the most successful examples of a previously little known European breed which is now spreading internationally is probably the Swiss laufhund. It has become so popular outside its home country, notably in Norway, that the Swiss may soon have to go abroad to find a representative selection of their own breed.

The Swiss laufhund is an active, friendly dog of powerful build. Features of the head are the prominent occipital bone, the marked stop (with a pronounced furrow in the middle), the dark and slightly slanting eyes and the large, thin and supple ears. The ears, a key characteristic of the breed, are lower set than in most other breeds of similar type. The legs are well boned and the thick tail is carried high in action. The coat is smooth and short.

The colour is predominantly white with lemon or orange patches. Height at shoulder should be at least 16in, but varies considerably.

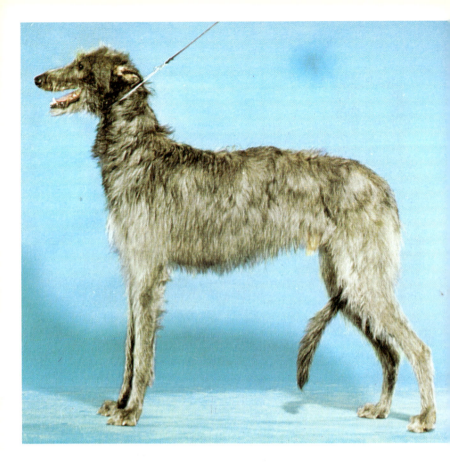

151 Deerhound *Scotland*

When firearms replaced the dog as a means of dispatching the huntsman's prey and when several species of larger game were drastically reduced in numbers as a result, the deerhound was threatened with extinction. However, the breed was nurtured among a few of the clans in the Scottish Highlands and today has a small but faithful following throughout the world.

For a long time, the deerhound and the Irish wolfhound (78) were largely varieties of the same type of dog and the two breeds could not be properly distinguished until the nineteenth century. Today, however, they are easy to tell apart: even though the deerhound may often be as tall as the wolfhound, it is always considerably lighter and more graceful in build and possesses the distinct characteristics of the sighthound. The deerhound can more accurately be described as a wire–haired greyhound. In temperament it is usually docile and friendly.

It is built on racy lines with a wiry, shaggy, blue-grey coat, dark eyes, small thin black ears and a tail which almost reaches the ground. Height at shoulder is at least 30in for dogs, and at least 28in for bitches. Weight is 85–105lb and 65–80lb respectively.

152 Appenzell Mountain Dog
(Appenzeller Sennenhund)

The smooth-coated Appenzell mountain dog is one of four breeds used extensively at one time as herding dogs on the Alpine slopes of Switzerland. The breed originates and takes its name from a canton in northern Switzerland. In its home area it is very common—there is even a breed club—but it is rare outside Switzerland.

The Appenzell mountain dog is of a similar type to the related, but more common, Bernese mountain dog, but it is usually much smaller and more rectangular in build. The head is broad, the ears carried close to the head and the body muscular and sturdy. The coat, as distinct from the Bernese mountain dog, is smooth, and the tail—more thickly covered with hair than the rest of the body—is curled over the back.

The colour is black with tan and white markings on the head, legs and chest; the tip of the tail is always white. Height at shoulder is usually about 20in.

153 Bernese Mountain Dog
(Berner Sennenhund)

Many people would say that the Bernese mountain dog looks like 'a real dog' and it undoubtedly conjures up the children's picture-book conception of 'man's best friend'. There is nothing extreme about its lines, just a well balanced creature with an air of friendliness—a dog of the old school.

The Bernese mountain dog was hardly known outside its homeland, Switzerland, until more recent times and it has now exchanged the role of sheepdog for family pet. It bears an unmistakable resemblance to the St Bernard (144), but though they have a common origin, the Bernese mountain dog has existed as an independent breed just as long as its larger relative.

The Bernese mountain dog is strong, powerful and agile. The head is broad, the eyes dark brown and the ears carried close to the head. The coat is profuse, close and fairly soft.

The colour is black with smaller tan markings on the fore-face and legs, a white blaze on the head and a white 'shirt front'. Height at shoulder is 25–28in for dogs, 23–26in for bitches.

Switzerland

154 Entlebuch Mountain Dog
(Entlebucher Sennenhund)

Like other Swiss 'sennen' dogs, the Entlebuch mountain dog
has evolved as a result of deliberate attempts in modern times
to preserve an old breed type.

For a long time the breed was almost extinct, until a Swiss
travelling salesman, fascinated by the unusual type, collected
all the remaining animals he could find and managed to re-
awaken interest among local people in what was their own,
local variety of dog. Thus the breed survived. It was not officially recognised as a breed until well into this century, and
though it is popular in its native country it has remained
very rare in most others.

The Entlebuch mountain dog is the smallest of the four
Swiss 'sennen' breeds and is of a similar type, though it bears
a particularly close resemblance to the variety from Appenzell. It has a broad skull, dark eyes and the ears, which are
proportionately larger than those of the Bernese mountain
dog, are carried close to the head. The neck is shorter and
thicker, the body longer and the legs considerably shorter
than those of its close relatives. The tail is short.

The colour is black with tan and white markings on the
head, chest and legs. Height at shoulder is 16–20in.

185

155 Large Swiss Mountain Dog
(Grosser Schweizer Sennenhund)

As distinct from the other 'sennen' breeds, the large Swiss mountain dog is not a local variety but was spread throughout Switzerland at an early stage. Its purpose, too, was slightly different: it was mainly used as a cattle dog when driving the herds to the market in the days before the railway existed. For this task it needed to be slightly larger and heavier than its relatives. The large Swiss mountain dog is not very common outside its home country.

It is the largest of the Swiss cattle and herding breeds, slightly taller than the Bernese mountain dog and altogether heavier and sturdier. The ears are larger than those of the Bernese mountain dog and carried dropped, the neck is long, thick and muscular. The body is broad, deep and muscular and the tail fairly long and carried low.

The colour is that of the other 'sennen' breeds: predominantly black with tan markings on the head, chest and legs, a white blaze on the foreface, white throat and feet.

Height at shoulder is 25–28in for dogs, 23–26in for bitches.

Great Britain

156 English Setter

A perfect English setter makes a handsome sight, but to
observe it only in the show ring does not do the breed
justice—it is seen to best advantage when working in the
field. It has altered hardly at all in type during two or three
centuries, though in more recent years a heavier type has
been evolved for the show ring in its native country. A lighter,
racier type is used for work in the shooting field.

It originated from English hunting spaniels and, as a result
of intensely selective breeding, was firmly established in the
mid-nineteenth century when for some time it was the leading
breed both at shows and in the field.

The English setter has an appearance of elegance, strength
and speed. The head is long with a fairly lean skull and a
marked stop, a straight, deep muzzle and expressive, dark
eyes. The back slopes towards the scimitar-shaped tail which
tapers off towards the tip. The long and glossy coat is particularly long on the ears chest, tail and on the back of the legs.

In colour, white predominates with markings in black,
lemon or liver; sometimes tricolour (black, white and tan).
Height at shoulder is about 25in.

Great Britain

157 Gordon Setter

At one time, the black and tan Gordon setter was the most popular of all pointing gundogs and in the early days of the setter varieties, about 1850, it won almost every class at dog shows as well as field trials. When the English setter appeared on the scene, the Gordon setter was displaced and has remained something of a rarity ever since.

The Gordon setter is slightly larger than the English setter and does not have quite the same elegant appearance. The ears are soft and lie close to the head. The tail does not reach below the hocks and in action is carried horizontally or below the line of the back. The coat is not very profuse, but forms long and silky featherings on the ears, belly, tail and back of the legs.

The colour is always black with smaller chestnut-red markings on the muzzle, chest and underside of the body. A white spot on the chest is allowed, but not desirable. Height at shoulder is about 26in for dogs and about 24in for bitches. Weight is around 60lb.

Great Britain

158 Irish Setter

The attractive rich chestnut colour of the Irish setter is such
a jealously preserved characteristic of the breed that over a
century ago the Irish formed a breed club to protect the pure
red colour from any intermingling of blood from particoloured dogs.

Unfortunately, the latter type proved to be more useful
as gundogs and the preference of the Irish for a pure red
dog meant that their setter became less widely used than the
particoloured dogs. But the Irish setter has retained its great
attraction and in recent years has outclassed even the English
setter (157), albeit in a different capacity and in another
country; in the USA it is now one of the most fashionable
show dogs.

By its striking colour and its dark, expressive eyes in combination with a lively and friendly temperament, the Irish
setter is possibly the most attractive of all the pointing gundog breeds. The coat is sleek, longer on the ears, chest, tail
and back of the legs.

The colour is always a glossy, rich chestnut with no trace
of other shades. Height at shoulder is usually about 24in and
weight around 55lb.

159 Shetland Sheepdog

The graceful little Shetland sheepdog with its neat looks, moderate size and usually affectionate and friendly temperament, is one of the most popular breeds among people seeking a pet. For centuries it has been used as a sheepdog on the Shetland Isles but it was not until the beginning of this century that the Sheltie's charm was discovered by the British; with characteristic promptness and energy they started at once on improvement and planned breeding.

The term 'minature collie' sometimes used to describe the Sheltie is considered quite unjustifiable by some breeders, although there is no doubt that collies were used to improve the breed.

The Shetland sheepdog is, above all, alert, intelligent and elegant. The head is virtually a smaller copy of that of the rough collie (39). The coat is profuse.

The colour is usually sable with white markings, but there are several other varieties. Height at shoulder is 14in for dogs, slightly less for bitches.

160 Shiba

The shiba is the smallest of the Japanese spitz breeds and, with the ainou (4) and the akita (5), one of the three main breeds within the group. Although it is undoubtedly an ancient breed originating from central Japan, it was not until 1928 that it was officially recognised in that country. Other Japanese spitz breeds are regarded in their native country as only local varieties of one of the three main types.

The shiba is used as a guard dog or companion, sometimes for hunting small game and birds. It has a rather short, broad skull with a pointed face and dark brown eyes, small triangular pricked ears, and a body that is deep without being too short. The coat is rough, coarse and straight. The tail may be curled, but a docked tail or a naturally bobbed tail is also acceptable. The colour is red, salt and pepper, black, black and tan or white. The temperament is markedly friendly.

Height at shoulder for dogs is 15–16in, 14–15in for bitches.

Tibet

161 Shih Tzu

It would be quite wrong to assume that the shih tzu, with its short legs and enormous coat, is the result of the fads and fancies of present day breeders. It is thought to have existed in the Tibetan highlands for at least two thousand years. It has obviously a great deal in common with the Pekingese, but today's European breeders are anxious that any interbreeding between the two should be avoided.

Like the Pekingese, this Tibetan toy dog was at one time used for religious ceremonies but, unlike its Chinese cousin, it acquired a very open and outgoing temperament. Today, and in spite of the grooming required for its profuse coat, it is one of the most popular of the smaller breeds.

The shih tzu is spirited and alert with a very long, thick and straight coat. The hair, which should not be curly, is particularly abundant on the head and ears and grows upwards on the nose, giving the head the typical 'chrysanthemum-like' effect.

All colours are acceptable, but a white blaze on the forehead and a white tip to the tail are highly prized. Height at shoulder varies considerably, but is preferably just under 12in. Weight is up to 18lb, but ideally 9–16lb.

Siberia

162 Siberian Husky

For centuries, the Siberian husky has been kept as a household companion–a role not enjoyed by other Arctic spitz breeds until modern times. It has also been used by the Siberian nomads for such utilitarian tasks as sledhauling or herding. The breed's long association with man has made the Siberian husky comparatively more 'civilised' and more spontaneously friendly towards humans than other Arctic spitz breeds. It was officially recognised as a breed by the American Kennel Club at the beginning of this century.

The Siberian husky is both powerful and elegant. The head is typical of the spitz, with erect ears and an alert expression, but the tail need not be carried as tightly curled over the back as in most other spitz breeds; when the dog is at rest, the tail is dropped. The coat is thick, fairly long, hangs loosely from the body and is surprisingly soft to the touch.

The colour is of little importance and all shades are acceptable. Most common is grey or light brown with white markings. Height at shoulder for dogs is 21–24in, 20–22in for bitches.

163 Sloughi

The sloughi is probably the rarest sighthound breed existing
in the West. It has sometimes been mistaken for a smooth
saluki (141), but it has certain characteristics which clearly
distinguish it from that breed. Its background, too, is different
from the saluki's. The sloughi is likely to have evolved in
Morocco as a result of the original Afro-Asian sighthound
spreading westwards along the coast of North Africa. The
ruling class of Morocco adopted it and produced the sloughi
type in their kennels. Since then, the sloughi has been allowed
to intermingle with other breeds and animals from the pure–
bred strains must now be very rare.

In conformation, the sloughi differs from the saluki by its
slightly heavier build and the frequently occurring black
'spectacle' markings around the eyes.

The colour is usually sandy, sometimes brindle. Height at
shoulder is 22–30in.

164 Slovakian Kuvasz (Slovensky Čuvač)

The Slovakian kuvasz is thought to have originated from the slightly more common kuvasz of Hungary (87), but it bears just as close a resemblance to the Polish owczarek podhalanski (114). These three breeds could be said to be local varieties in their respective countries of the same herding breed. Both the Polish and the Slovakian breeds sometimes go under the name of Tatry dogs, after the mountain range which stretches through both countries and where the two breeds have existed for a long time.

Despite its smaller stature, the Slovakian kuvasz is almost as imposing as its close relatives. It is heavily boned, has a lively temperament and is alert, brave and intelligent. Its name is probably derived from the Slovakian word for hearing.

Originally only white animals were bred in order that the dog could be easily distinguished from beasts of prey in the darkness. Pure white is still the most desirable colour, though an off-white shade is acceptable. Other colours are, however, severely penalised.

Height at shoulder is around 24in, but should not exceed 28in for dogs, 26in for bitches.

165 Slovakian Kopov
(Slovensky Kopov)

The Czechoslovakian hound, the Slovakian kopov, is the only hunting breed of its kind in its home country. It is descended from a variety of different hounds which existed several hundred years ago in Czechoslovakia, and over the centuries has evolved as a distinct type. It has a reputation for toughness and agility.

It is of medium size and of robust, slightly thick-set build. The head is long, the jaws powerful and the ears fairly large and carried close to the head. The length of the kopov's back, which is level, is greater than its height at the shoulder. The tail is thick, of medium length and well covered with coarse hair, but not forming a fringe. The coat is 1–2in long.

The colour is black with brown markings above the eyes, on the cheeks, feet, the lower parts of the legs and around the vent. Height at shoulder for dogs is 18–20in, 16–18in for bitches.

166 American Cocker Spaniel

The American cocker spaniel is an interesting example of what can happen when a breed moves from one country to another. When the British began to colonise America they introduced spaniels which gradually, and without any mixture of strange blood, managed to become so different and 'American' in type that, towards the end of the last century, they were eventually officially recognised as a separate breed. This more extreme and showy spaniel variety has been popular as a pet for a long time in America but only in recent years has it gained ground in Scandinavia and Great Britain.

The American cocker spaniel is usually slightly smaller than the English variety (170) and is strikingly compactly built. The coat, which is either straight or wavy, is much more profuse than that of the ordinary cocker, especially on the ears, legs and belly.

The colour varies from self-colours to particolours or roans in any shades. Weight is around 22–28lb and height at shoulder is around 15in.

167 American Water Spaniel

The American relative of the Irish water spaniel (173) is considerably smaller than its ancestor. Its exact origin is unknown, but it is believed that the Irish water spaniel was crossed with smaller, American spaniel breeds which resulted in a dog which became particularly popular in the southern states. In many areas it is still known as the Boykin spaniel after a town in South Carolina. Two or three hundred puppies are registered yearly in the USA, but the American water spaniel is almost unknown outside its home country. It was not officially recognised as a breed until 1940.

In the main, the breed is a smaller copy of its Irish relative. It is, however, slightly longer in body and has a broader skull. As distinct from its relative, the tail is covered with hair right to the tip. The coat is tightly curled.

The colour is liver or chocolate brown. Small white markings on toes and chest are acceptable. Height at shoulder is 15–18in.

168 Cavalier King Charles Spaniel

The affectionate Cavalier King Charles spaniel has a royal history going back several hundred years. At the English Court it was for long a great favourite, especially during the reign of Charles II. It is said that the King never went anywhere without being surrounded by his collection of small, happy toy spaniels.

In the nineteenth century, when everything oriental became fashionable, the Cavalier King Charles spaniel was crossed with the short-nosed toy breeds which were imported from China and Japan and for a time was in danger of disappearing as a pure breed. Officially, the Cavalier is a fairly new breed and was not recognised in its home country until the 1940s. It has since gained a large and faithful following as a breed which is, above all, engaging, docile and friendly.

In conformation, the Cavalier resembles an old hunting spaniel in minature: it is active, graceful, spirited and sturdily built.

There are four colour varieties: black and tan (pure black with small brown markings), Blenheim (white with chestnut red markings and a white blaze on the forehead), tricolour (black and white with small tan markings) and ruby (a whole-coloured rich red). The breed standard does not specify height at shoulder. The weight is 10–18lb.

169 Clumber Spaniel

The clumber spaniel has been advertised as the breed for the individualist, for people who don't like transistor radios and the other new-fangled things of modern life—and it is true that the clumber spaniel has something of old-fashioned dignity about it. It had its heyday towards the end of the nineteenth century when it was regularly used as a gundog by the British aristocracy. It is very rare outside Great Britain.

According to the breed standard, the clumber is a heavy and massive dog with a thoughtful expression. As a gundog breed it also needs to be active. The head is large and square with a broad skull and pronounced occiput. The muzzle is heavy and deep with a flesh-coloured nose, the eyes are dark and the ears large and vine-leaf shaped. The body is long and heavy and the legs short, very well boned and strong. The tail is short, the coat close, silky and straight. The legs, tail and belly (but not the ears) are well feathered.

The colour is white with smaller lemon markings. Weight varies from 45–70lb.

170 Cocker Spaniel

Its melting expression, long ears, incessant wagging tail and, not least, its merry and affectionate temperament, have made the cocker spaniel one of the most popular breeds in the world.

It is, in fact, a gundog and though it is generally kept as a pet it usually manages to find some suitable outlet for its boundless energy. Although the spaniel type is ancient in Great Britain, the cocker was not recognised as a breed until just before the turn of this century. It did not gain its present vast popularity until after World War II.

The cocker spaniel is an active little sporting dog with a friendly, trusting disposition. The head is cleanly chiselled with flat cheeks and a marked stop. The eyes are full and of a colour harmonising with the coat. The ears are low-set, long and supple. The body is compact and deep, the legs well boned with round feet. The tail is docked fairly short, is carried low and incessantly active. The coat is smooth and silky with long, soft feathering on the ears, chest and on the back of the legs.

The colour may vary from solid colours to particolours or roans (white speckled with black, lemon, orange or liver). Ideal height at shoulder is about 16in.

171 English Springer Spaniel *Great Britain*

Despite its more robust size and calmer temperament, the English springer spaniel has not become as popular as the cocker (170). One of the reasons for this may be its less distinctive appearance, but the fact that the springer has been kept for hunting much more than the cocker has undoubtedly had an effect. One should really compare the English springer with the setters rather than the cocker, since the springer is considerably taller and more long-legged than the cocker, and has smaller ears.

Setters and spaniels are descended from the same type of gundog but while setters became established as a type fairly quickly, weight was the only deciding factor in distinguishing cockers from springers up to the end of the last century.

The English springer spaniel is a medium-sized, strong and active dog. The colour of the eyes and the nose harmonises with the coat colour. The ears are large but not as long as the cocker's and are set higher. The tail is low set, often with a lively action. The coat is short and glossy on the body and head, and thick, fairly long and slightly wavy on the ears, chest, under the body and on the back of the legs.

The colour is usually white with black or liver markings. Height at shoulder for dogs is about 20in; bitches are slightly smaller.

172 Field Spaniel

The field spaniel is rarely exhibited at dog shows in its home country; one normally has to attend field trials to see it since it has remained a working breed. It is shown more in the USA where, incidentally, there is a native, slightly smaller variety of the breed. The field spaniel, of course, shares the ancestry of the other spaniel breeds.

It is a well balanced sporting dog with a very docile temperament. According to the breed standard it also has a 'grave' expression. The head is similar to the cocker's (170), but is not as distinctive and is really more like a setter's. The body and bone are lighter than the cocker's and the coat is less profuse, forming silky feathering similar to an Irish setter's (158).

As in most other spaniel breeds, there are several colour varieties, but black, black and tan, roan or solid-colour shades of liver are considered more desirable than particolours. Height at shoulder is about 18in.

173 Irish Water Spaniel

One may forgive the layman for mistaking the Irish water spaniel for a poodle (31). Though the water spaniel lacks the sophisticated elegance which is the hall-mark of the poodle, the two breeds still have a great deal in common–the poodle was, after all, once used as a water retriever.

The Irish water spaniel has evolved from several different types of spaniel which were common in Ireland and Scotland at the end of the nineteenth century. Although it was recognised as a breed earlier than most other gundogs in Britain, it has remained fairly rare.

The Irish water spaniel is strongly built, eager and intelligent. The coat is an important characteristic: it has a natural oiliness and is composed of thick, tight ringlets—profuse everywhere except on the muzzle, just above the eyes and on the tail, where the ringlets stop abruptly a few inches below the root.

The colour is always a dark liver with a purplish tint. Height at shoulder for dogs is about 21–23in, 20–22in for bitches.

Great Britain

174 King Charles Spaniel

The King Charles spaniel was highly popular for a time, particularly in Britain, and much more common than its close relative the Cavalier King Charles spaniel (168). Now the position is reversed. Two points should be remembered when considering these related breeds: the Cavalier is true to the original British type, and the King Charles spaniel hardly justifies its name in any way.

It is true that Charles II, after whom the breed is named, did keep toy spaniels, but the interbreeding with East Asian toy dogs which created the King Charles spaniel did not start until a century and a half after his time. Nowadays, there is not much spaniel blood left in the breed. Despite its irresistibly superior expression and its fairly quiet disposition, it is relatively rare in most countries.

The King Charles spaniel differs from the Cavalier King Charles spaniel mainly by its flat nose and, frequently, by its more manageable size.

There are four colour varieties: black and tan, Blenheim (white and chestnut), tricolour (white, black and tan) and ruby (whole-coloured rich red). The breed standard does not specify height. Weight is around 8–14lb.

175 Sussex Spaniel

The heavy, sturdy and docile Sussex spaniel is one of the real rarities—not common anywhere in the world, not even in its native country. It has existed as an established breed since the eighteenth century, although it has altered a little over the years. With so few animals available for breeding, it was occasionally necessary to resort to outcrosses to avoid too much inbreeding. The clumber spaniel (169) was one of the breeds introduced in this process and this accounts for the fairly similar conformation of the two breeds.

The Sussex spaniel is bulky and muscular but not quite as heavy as the clumber. The eyes have a soft, slightly wistful expression. The ears are thicker than in most other spaniels, but not very large. The back is long and level, the legs strong and muscular. The tail is docked, but not too short; it is well feathered with hair and carried low. The coat is abundant and sleek with feathering on the legs, ears and thighs.

The colour is liver, shading to gold at the tips—a characteristic feature of the breed. The weight is about 45lb. Height at shoulder is 15–16in.

Tibet

176 Tibetan Spaniel

Several varieties of toy dogs existed in ancient Tibet—and reputedly still do—which fulfilled various purposes at religious ceremonies. With neither kennel clubs nor dog shows in existence, division into 'breeds' in any real sense had to wait until the little Tibetan dogs were brought to the West.

The variety now called the Tibetan spaniel differs considerably from the others and could, with certain reservations, be described most closely as something between a Pekingese (118) and a shih tzu (161). Although several attempts have been made to introduce the breed to many countries, it has remained fairly rare.

The Tibetan spaniel is elegant and fairly long in body. The head is domed and the muzzle short, but not flat. The ears are dropped like the Pekingese's, but the eyes are not as large and prominent and the legs are longer and straighter. The tail is carried in a plume over the back and the coat, though similar to the Pekingese's, is not quite as profuse.

Many colours are acceptable: white, cream, fawn, golden, brown or black—whole colours or particolours. Height at shoulder for dogs should not exceed 11in or about 9in for bitches.

177 Welsh Springer Spaniel

Spaniels are believed to have existed in Wales for many centuries and the Welshman's traditional suspicion of the English probably accounts for the fact that the type of spaniel which was evolved in the Principality has remained practically free from foreign blood for two hundred years. It does, nonetheless, fairly closely resemble the English Springer spaniel (171).

The Welsh springer spaniel was not recognised as a separate breed by the Kennel Club until this century. It is not yet very common anywhere in the world.

It is spirited, strong, active and built for endurance and hard work. The head, which is neither short nor chubby, differs from the English springer's mainly by its shorter ears. The eyes are hazel or dark brown, the nose flesh-coloured or black. The body is strong and muscular, the feet small and cat-like and the tail is low-set and carried low. The coat is smooth, thick and silky but not too profuse and with moderate feathering on the ears and back of the legs.

The colour is always white with dark rich red markings. Weight is around 35–45lb and height at shoulder about 16in.

178 Spinone *Italy*

Although the Italian spinone—the Italian pointer—has a great deal more in common with the pointer (127) from Britain than just the name, it surpasses it in versatility. It is, for one thing, reputedly used for tracking game. It is descended from the old European hunting dogs, the griffons, which have contributed to the blood lines of so many of today's gundog breeds. In the field, the spinone lacks the pointer's speed and is considered to be fairly heavy-footed.

In conformation, the Italian pointer is slightly heavier and coarser than the English pointer. The head is large with a fairly broad and domed skull, the stop is not very accentuated, but the muzzle is well developed and square. The nose is brown, light brown or liver with well expanded nostrils. The ears are large and carried close to the head. The eyes under the bushy eyebrows are light brown or yellow and they have an alert expression. The back is slightly arched over the loin and the chest is deep but not broad. The feet are round and the toes well knuckled up. The tail is carried in line with, or slightly above, the back. The coat is fairly short, hard and wiry.

The spinone is either pure white, or white with small lemon or light brown markings. Height at shoulder varies considerably from 24–28in for dogs to 23–26in for bitches.

179 Stabyhoun

The stabyhoun is one of the rarer pointing gundogs. Its looks are unpretentious, but it is reputed to be easily trained and very pleasing as a pet. Its origin is not quite clear, but its close links with the other Dutch gundogs are obvious.

The stabyhoun is of rectangular build and is neither very graceful nor heavy. The eyes are dark in black roan types and may be lighter in other colour varieties, but never yellow. The tail is long and well feathered, the lower third curving upwards. The coat is long and flat without curl.

The colour is usually white with black, blue, liver or orange markings. Height at shoulder should not exceed 20in for dogs; bitches should be about 1in smaller.

180 Dunkerstövare

It would be impossible to launch into the history of the Norwegian dunkerstövare without including the hygenhund (183). Originally, the two were entirely different in type. As the dunkerstövare type began to diminish in numbers there was a risk of close inbreeding resulting, so the strangely coloured grey roan dunkerstövare was crossed with the hygenhund and the two breeds merged. Even though still officially regarded as separate breeds there is very little, except colour, by which one can tell them apart. Outside their home country, Norway, both breeds are fairly rare.

The dunkerstövare is a powerful dog with great stamina and a grave expression. The head is fairly long with a marked stop, a straight foreface and usually dark eyes; light colour eyes are, however, acceptable in piebald varieties. The ears are carried close to the head. The tail, which should be as straight as possible, reaches the hock. The coat is coarse, thick and close.

The colour is black or piebald (black and grey) with white, brown or fawn markings. Height at shoulder is 18–23in.

Norway

181 Haldenstövare

As distinct from most other Scandinavian harrier/foxhound type breeds, the Haldenstövare stems mainly from British rather than continental imports. Foxhounds from Britain in combination with native Norwegian varieties have merged with this, the most 'modern' of all the hounds tracking by scent; it was not recognised as a breed until the 1950s. The resemblance to the foxhound (58) is still very strong, but the Haldenstövare is usually slightly smaller than its British ancestor.

It is heavily built with an unexcitable disposition. The head bears close resemblance to the foxhound's, with a slightly tapering foreface and large, soft ears. The eyes are dark brown, the neck long and the body strong and powerful. Dewclaws (rudimentary claws on the inside of the pastern) are acceptable. The tail is thick, but is carried lower than the foxhound's.

The colour is usually white with black patches and smaller tan markings on the head and the legs. Height at shoulder is 20–24in.

182 Hamiltonstövare

The Hamiltonstövare can safely be called the most popular Swedish hunting breed. It is not as numerically strong as the drever (53) but while the latter is an almost unchanged Swedish version of a German breed, the Hamiltonstövare has for centuries been bred specifically for Swedish hunting conditions. It is rare in other countries. The Hamiltonstövare also originates from foreign hounds—mainly imports from Britain, Germany and Switzerland.

It is a powerful, agile dog with great stamina. The head is cleanly cut with a full, fairly long foreface. The eyes are clear and dark brown. The ears are fairly large and soft and are carried close to the head. The tail is either straight or very slightly wavy. The coat is close and weather-resistant.

The Hamiltonstövare is always tricolour: tan predominates, with a black saddle and white markings on the muzzle, throat, chest, feet and tip of the tail. Height at shoulder for dogs is 20–24in, 18–22in for bitches.

Norway

183 Hygenhund

(Stövare, Hygenhund)

Formerly the Norwegian hygenhund was a distinct breed commonly found in the midlands and eastern parts of Norway. However, even before the end of the last century the breed was so interbred with the dunkerstövare that the two are now almost indistinguishable. Originally the hygenhund was red fawn in colour, but since interbreeding with the dunkerstövare, a black variety is not uncommon.

The main difference between black types of the two breeds is held to be that the hygenhund is slightly heavier and less elegant. The head is broad with a marked stop and a wide foreface, which is slightly shorter than the dunkerstövare's. The colour of the eyes should harmonise with the coat colour, but the hygenhund should never have light colour eyes. The ears are thin and supple, the coat thick, flat and glossy.

The colour varies: tan, black and tan, or white with tan and/or black markings are all acceptable. Height at shoulder is 19–24in.

Sweden

184 Schillerstövare

Although not as numerous at the Hamiltonstövare, the schillerstövare is one of Sweden's most commonly used hounds for locating and tracking game. It is generally found in the western parts of the country. Despite its resemblance to the Hamiltonstövare, the schillerstövare springs, in part, from different hunting dog ancestry. Its forebears were mostly dogs imported from southern Germany, Austria and Switzerland, and as these animals were already fairly even in type, making further out-crossing unnecessary, the schillerstövare evolved as a breed before the currently more ubiquitous Hamiltonstövare.

The main difference between the two breeds is that the schillerstövare is slightly lighter than the Hamiltonstövare, without appearing spindly in any way. The head is fairly long with a marked stop, dark luminous eyes, and supple ears which are carried close to the head. The neck is long and strong, the body powerful with a deep chest. The tail is straight or sabre-shaped, the coat close and short.

The colour is always tan with a black saddle. White markings, except possibly a trace on the chest or toes, are not acceptable. Dogs stand 20–24in at the shoulder, bitches 18–23in.

185 Smålandsstövare

Though not recognised as a breed by the Swedish Kennel Club until the 1920s, the Smålandsstövare possibly represents the oldest type of hound used in Sweden for tracking and locating game. The breed gets its name from the county of Småland, the area where dogs of this type were probably first used for this purpose. As breed standards, registers and breed control are modern ideas, the Smålandsstövares of old were a very mixed collection. It was not until after 1900 that any real attempts were made to get a more uniform type, but today the breed has its own characteristics which clearly distinguish it from other varieties.

The Smålandsstövare is an active and agile dog and should be strongly built but not heavy. The foreface is neither broad nor sharp and the eyes are dark with a tranquil expression. The ears, which are carried close to the head, are soft and rounded at the tips. The tail is either short (by nature), or long and reaching the hock; it is either straight or slightly curved.

The colour is black with tan markings above the eyes, on the feet and under the tail. Dogs stand about 20in at the shoulder, bitches 18in.

186 Finnish Stövare
(Suomenajokoira)

The ancestry of the Finnish stövare is highly mixed. In addition to the old hunting dogs—which also fathered the Swedish 'stövare' varieties—there are other imported ancestors, notably from Russia. The type as we know it today was not finally evolved until the 1930s.

As the type of the Finnish stövare was developed before the Scandinavian varieties, it has had time to become more established in Scandinavian countries than other breeds of similar type. The layman may easily mistake it for the Hamiltonstövare (182), but as well as a few other differences, the Finnish stövare is usually a fraction taller and slightly more rectangular in build.

The Finnish stövare is powerful without being heavy and has a very docile, yet alert, temperament. The occiput is more pronounced than in the Hamiltonstövare; the foreface is long, strong and finely chiselled. The eyes are dark and the ears carried close to the head. The tail reaches approximately to the hock; the coat is close and fairly hard.

The colour is tan with a black saddle and white markings on the foreface, neck, chest, feet and tip of the tail.

Finland

187 Finnish Spitz (Suomenpystykorva)

The Finnish spitz is a lively hunter whose main function is to flush game-birds up into the trees and keep them there until the shooting party arrives. Its ancestors have existed throughout the Scandinavian countries since prehistoric time. The first Finnish spitz breed standard was drawn up by the Finns in the last century and the breed has since improved in type and for hunting. Recently it has become popular as a pet outside Scandinavia, especially in Britain.

The Finnish spitz has all the spitz characteristics: a firmly knit body, bold bearing, a lively temperament—and the ability to make itself heard! The eyes sparkle with eagerness to hunt and the ears are mobile, cocked and sharply pointed. The body is short and lithe, the legs straight with a springy action and the tail curves vigorously in an arch against the thigh. The coat is profuse, fairly long and very straight and is particularly long on the neck, back, tail and thighs.

The colour is a bright reddish-brown or yellowish-red with lighter shadings—preferably without a narrow white stripe on the breast or white markings on the feet. Particolours are not acceptable. Height at shoulder is 17–20in for dogs, 15–18in for bitches.

188 Japanese Chin
(Tchin)

It is strange that this elegant little toy breed from the East
has not become more popular. It is dainty and attractive,
lively and very affectionate. For over a thousand years it was
a favourite at the court of the Japanese emperors and came
to Europe with returning seamen in medieval times. For a
short period the Japanese chin was very popular in Britain
but today breeding is on a smaller scale. New blood from
its country of origin is said to be impossible to obtain.

The Japanese chin has a great deal in common with the
Chinese Pekingese and is thought to have evolved from common stock. The Japanese toy dog is, however, taller on the
leg with a lighter body and graceful, high-stepping movement.
The head is fairly large and rounded with a flat nose and
a slight 'furrow' on the upper lip. The eyes are large and
dark with the whites clearly showing at the inner corners.
The coat is profuse and long, free from curl, and particularly
abundant on the tail, thighs, front legs and feet.

The colour is always white with evenly distributed patches
in black or a shade of red. Size varies and though the smaller
the better, it may have a height at shoulder of up to 11in.

Germany

189 Smooth-haired Dachshund
(Kurzhaariger Teckel)

A completely impartial observer might well wonder why the dachshund is one of the most popular breeds in Europe—but who can possibly be impartial as far as dachshunds are concerned? The dachshund is no great beauty, it lacks the impressive substance of the bull breeds, the refined elegance of the poodles and the trainability of the working, guard and police dogs. The reason for its popularity can be found in its many-sided personality: friendliness which is not cajoling, exuberance tempered by common sense and faithfulness mixed with a good portion of obstinacy—which other breeds merit such a description?

Early research tended to credit the breed with a history even longer than that to which it is entitled and claimed origins going back to ancient Egyptian and South American cultures. Although this suggests a somewhat exaggerated zeal,

Germany

190 Long-haired Dachshund
(Langhaariger Teckel)

it is a fact that short-legged dogs, ancestors of the dachshund, existed in southern Germany well over a thousand years ago. Naturally, the type has changed considerably over the centuries.

Its speciality in the early days, as now, was hunting under ground—as far as one can talk about a speciality for such a versatile breed, which is just as frequently used for tracking game or driving it to the guns. However, most dachshunds today are more likely to be kept as pets even though in Europe and in Scandinavia they are keen to preserve its excellent qualities as a hunting dog.

There has been lively discussion about how the division into different sizes and coat textures came about. Dachshunds of all types, however, evolved through mutations several hundred years ago, but while the smooth-haired and long-

191 Wire-haired Dachshund
(Rauhhaariger Teckel)

haired types quickly gained popularity, the wire-haired variety was gradually pushed into the background and, for a
time, disappeared. It was not until the end of the nineteenth
century that attempts were made to revive the wire, and
schnauzers and Dandie Dinmont terriers were used, among
others, as outcrosses. The methods used were successful and
the wires today are of as high a quality as the other coat
varieties.

There are two smaller versions of the dachshund: the
miniature dachshund and an even smaller type known in
some countries as the 'rabbit' dachshund with measurements
around the girth not exceeding 14in and 12in respectively.
These miniatures evolved in Germany at the turn of this century, mainly through crosses between the smallest of the stan-

Germany

192 Miniature Long-haired Dachshund
(Langhaariger Zwergteckel)

dard varieties, but other small breeds were also used. The miniatures as well as the 'rabbit' dachshunds can be either wire-haired, smooth-haired or long-haired.

The dachshund is active, bold and alert. It is short-legged with a long body and proud carriage. The head is long and well chiselled and tapers gradually to the nose. The eyes are almond-shaped and should not be lighter than chestnut brown. The ears are rounded and lie close to the cheek. The neck is long and moderately arched, the back long and slightly curved over the loin, the legs short, straight and well boned.

The colour varies from black and tan, to red, chocolate, brindle and dapple. A standard dachshund of average size should weigh not more than 20lb.

193 Airedale Terrier

With its majestic serenity and imposing size the Airedale terrier is unique within the terrier group, which mainly comprises small, lively dogs. The reason for its very special type can be traced to the kennels which were established several hundred years ago in the large foxhunting districts. The small hunting terriers then kept were occasionally crossed with foxhounds. The result was a versatile dog combining the stubbornness and courage of the terrier with the good nose and hunting instinct of the hound. In some countries, the Airedale is used as a working dog.

It has the appearance of both power and elegance. The head is long with a flat skull, flat cheeks and very powerful jaws and teeth. The eyes are small, dark brown and full of terrier expression in combination with calm confidence. The coat is hard and wiry with a soft undercoat. The ears are small and folded, and carried to the side of the head.

The colour on the head and legs is a warm tan, with black or dark grizzle on the rest of the body. Dogs stand about 24in at the shoulder, slightly less for bitches. Weight is usually around 55lb.

194 American Toy Terrier

The American toy terrier was stabilised as a type just after the turn of this century, but is not officially recognised as a separate breed. Despite this, it is very popular as a pet and thousands are bred every year. It is descended from the fox terrier (207) but bears the stamp of various toy breeds.

The American toy terrier resembles a small smooth fox terrier but is much finer in bone and has pricked ears. The head is more pointed and the jaws weaker. The tail is docked fairly short and is carried erect.

The colour is usually white, with black or black and tan markings. A typical 'miniature fox terrier' should not exceed 8–9lb in weight, preferably not more than 4–4½lb.

195 Australian Terrier

As its name indicates, the Australian terrier does not originate directly from Britain, but as it stems from British stock exported to Australia it could be described as a British breed. Emigrants to Australia were mostly British and took their terriers with them from home; these dogs, all different varieties, eventually produced the conglomerate out of which the Australian terrier breed was born.

It is not known exactly which terrier breeds were involved to produce the breed, but there is no doubt that the original Yorkshire terrier played a leading part.

The Australian terrier is a rather low-set, active little dog with a keen expression in its dark eyes. The ears are small, pricked or dropped forwards. The neck has a decided frill of longer hair.

The colour is dark blue or silver grey with rich tan markings on the head and the legs. Height at shoulder is about 10in and weight about 10–11lb.

196 Australian Silky Terrier

In some countries the Australian silky terrier belongs to the toy group while its older relative, the Australian terrier, is included in the terrier group. In many respects, however, there is so little separating the two breeds that one would prefer to have them classified under the same group heading; in fact this is the practice in some countries.

The Australian silky terrier emerged this century as a result of crosses between the Australian terrier and various other terrier and toy dog varieties, including the Yorkshire terrier (225) which is mainly responsible for two of the features separating the Australian terrier from the silky terrier. These are the silky terrier's fairly long, thick and silky coat, which is quite straight, and its body, which is more compact and shorter than the Australian terrier's. The silky terrier is slightly smaller than the Australian terrier and stands about 9in at the shoulder.

197 Bedlington Terrier

The Bedlington readily attracts attention by its original and elegant, sophisticated appearance. Many find it difficult to believe that this really is a terrier. It does, however, originate from the old wire-haired terriers which were used for hunting fox and badger in northern England, although it has also been crossed with sighthounds, among others.

As keen a temperament as possible was aimed for and even today it may be referred to as 'a wolf in sheep's clothing'. Even though the breed has grown considerably more tractable since the nineteenth century, it is certainly not as meek as it appears. It is a dog full of spirit and courage.

The Bedlington terrier is graceful and lithe with a light, dainty action. The head is very narrow seen from above and completely lacks a stop. The coat could be most closely described as a soft, lint-like rug.

The colour is blue, liver or sandy with lighter shadings on the skull and ears. Height at shoulder is about 16in and weight between 18–23lbs.

198 Border Terrier

The Border terrier is not a flashy show dog, but is gaining ground as a robust, pleasant and manageable pet. As its name suggests, it hails from the rugged Border Country between England and Scotland. In this fairly isolated area a distinct type of dog evolved, bred exclusively for its ability to go to ground after fox or badger.

The Border terrier came into contact with dog shows and showdog breeding late in its development and is still one of the most natural and unspoiled of the terrier breeds.

The breed standard emphasises that the Border terrier is essentially a working terrier and must be both active and game. The head is otter-like with small, moderately thick ears dropping forward close to the cheek, and dark eyes with a bold, keen expression.

The colour is red, grizzle and tan, blue and tan or pure wheaten. Height at shoulder is usually about 10–12in and weight around 14lb.

199 Boston Terrier

The gay little Boston terrier is one of the breeds one would cheerfully recommend as a pet for anyone. Yet it descends from dogs which could not have been more unsuitable for family life. During the nineteenth century arranged dog fights were a national sport in Britain and the USA. Originally bulldogs and terriers were used but when someone hit on the idea of combining the strength of the bulldog with the tenacity of the terrier, the forerunner of the Boston terrier breed was born. Since then American and British breeders have reduced its size and made it a delightful and affectionate companion, without extinguishing the terrier spark. It has now spread and gained popularity nearly all over the world.

Although the Boston terrier is one of the smaller breeds, its compact body and stylish deportment demonstrate that it is determined, strong and active.

Brindle and white is the most desirable colour, but black and white is acceptable. Any other colour is unacceptable. Ideally there is a white blaze over the head, white muzzle, neck, chest, forelegs and hind legs below the hocks. Height at shoulder should not exceed 16in.

Great Britain

200 Bull Terrier

Comments about the bull terrier usually range from 'a dog just can't look like that' to admiring remarks about its 'sculptured beauty'. When bull baiting became illegal and the British started pitting dogs against each other instead, a type of dog was needed which was lither and quicker but just as strong and vicious as before: bulldogs were crossed with terriers and the result was a 'bull and terrier dog'. Other crosses were then made which gave the bull terrier its characteristic conformation and its more controllable temper.

It is strong and muscular without appearing clumsy. The head is a main feature: it is distinctly egg-shaped. The coat is short and glossy. The colour is white, brindle or coloured with white markings. There are neither weight nor height limits laid down in the breed standard, but height at shoulder is usually about 16in.

201 Bull Terrier, Miniature

One would have thought that the manageable miniature bull terrier would be just as popular as its larger brother, but it has not worked out that way. There are not more than a few of the type anywhere in the world, not even at the largest dog shows, and breeders are struggling to keep the quality of the breed reasonably in line with that of the more common bull terrier (200).

The ancestry is the same for both breeds and miniature varieties of the bull terrier have existed since the nineteenth century. In conformation, the miniature bull terrier is a smaller copy of the bull terrier but it is usually much less powerful throughout.

Height at shoulder must not exceed 14in, weight no more than 20lb.

202 Cairn Terrier

In the terrier country of Britain the Cairn terrier is now the breed which draws the biggest entries in the terrier group at dog shows. This lively and appealing breed is, understandably, very popular as a pet and companion.

The Cairn terrier comes from Inverness in Scotland. In its early days the breed had much in common with the Skye terrier and it was a fairly long time before its present name came into use: first known as the short-haired terrier and then as the West Highland terrier, it was accepted in 1910 by the Kennel Club as the Cairn terrier. The word 'cairn'—a pile of stones—comes from the Gaelic word for 'a heap'. It therefore makes a very appropriate name for a Scottish breed eager to 'go to ground'.

The Cairn terrier is an active and hardy little dog with a shaggy coat, a bold bearing and a somewhat fox-like expression.

The colour varies from sandy to nearly black. Darker shadings on ears and muzzle are very typical. Height at shoulder is about 10in, weight about 14lb.

Czechoslovakia

203 Cesky Terrier

The Cesky terrier is an extremely rare terrier breed, represented outside its home country by only a few animals—all directly descended from Czechoslovakian dogs.

In conformation, the Cesky terrier resembles something between the Kerry blue terrier and the sealyham; it is a sturdily-built, solid little dog, about the size of a sealyham and with similarly short legs. Cesky terriers so far exhibited outside their homeland seem to have a very pleasant temperament.

The colour is a blue grey or brown with lighter markings on the head, neck, chest and underside of the body. Acceptable height at shoulder is 11–14in.

204 Dandie Dinmont Terrier

An extraordinary silhouette in the terrier group! In most parts of the world the Dandie Dinmont terrier is regarded as a canine curiosity at dog shows, but in Britain it has had a fairly large following ever since it featured in Sir Walter Scott's novels at the beginning of the nineteenth century. Originally it was a wire-haired hunting terrier in the Cheviot Hills—the rugged border country between England and Scotland—but after its sudden climb to popularity it was bred to fit more easily into drawing-room life and hence got its present quaint looks.

The Dandie Dinmont terrier is a long and short dog with a large head profusely covered with soft and silky hair. The long body is low at the shoulders with an arch over the loins and a slight drop from the loin towards the root of the tail. The legs are short, the tail moderately long and carried in line with the back or slightly above it. The coat is a mixture of soft and fairly hard hair.

The colour ranges from a dark bluish black to a pale fawn. Height at shoulder is 8–11in and the ideal weight is about 18lb.

235

205 German Hunt Terrier
(Deutscher Jagdterrier)

The German hunt terrier is one of the few breeds within the terrier group which does not descend directly from Great Britain or Ireland. As yet it is extremely rare. As a breed, it is considerably less refined than its Anglo-Saxon cousins and should, according to the breed standard, be 'suspicious towards strangers'. In Germany it is used for a variety of hunting purposes, above and below ground, and even in water.

The German hunt terrier is more heavily built than any of the British terrier varieties. It should not be too short in the back, but a more rectangular appearance is desirable. Though the skull is flat, it is broader between the ears than, for example, the fox terrier (208). The jaws are powerful and the nose usually black, though it may blend with the coat in brown types. The eyes are deep-set and, according to the German breed standard, dark with a determined expression.

The coat is very thick, coarse and rough and the colour predominantly black, greyish black or dark brown with smaller, even markings. Some white on the chest is acceptable. Height at shoulder should not exceed 16in, while the weight for a dog in working condition is about 22lb, a few pounds less for bitches.

Great Britain

206 English Toy Terrier

Today it may be difficult to see that the English toy terrier has anything in common with the other terrier breeds, but in fact it is descended from the old smooth-coated breed, the Manchester terrier, which for centuries was used for ratting in northern England. There is also a measure of sighthound blood and today the breed could be said to stand somewhere between the two groups. The toy variety is of a later date than the Manchester terrier; it did not evolve until the nineteenth century and is still not very popular.

The English toy terrier is elegantly and cleanly built and, according to the breed standard, it should be built to be able to perform in the rat pit. The head is flat and narrow with small eyes, set fairly close together and with a keen, sparkling expression. The ears are erect. The tail is fairly long and thin and should not be carried above the level of the back. The coat is short and glossy.

The colour is always black with chestnut-coloured markings, which should be evenly distributed on the muzzle, cheeks and the inside of the legs.

Height at shoulder is 10–12in, and ideal weight is 6–8lb.

207 Fox Terrier, Smooth

The smooth fox terrier is of a slightly later date than its wire-haired relative and is believed to have sprung from crosses between wire-haired terriers and, among others, dogs used for fox hunting. In temperament, too, it usually differs: the smooth is considered to be less temperamental and more restrained than the wire.

In popularity, it has never quite achieved the pinnacles of the wire but, on the other hand, its following has been more steady and constant. Today smooth fox terriers are often more numerous at dog shows than wires.

Very little separates the two varieties as far as conformation is concerned and the same breed standard largely applies. The head, however, is slightly more tapering from the ears towards the eyes and the muzzle is slightly more pointed, without being sharp. The coat should be smooth, thick and close. The belly and underside of the thighs should not be bare.

Colour, height and weight are the same as for the wire fox terrier.

208 Fox Terrier, Wire

The wire fox terrier is often regarded as *the* terrier, partly because it led the field in popularity over a number of years and partly because, both in temperament and conformation, it has all the characteristic terrier features: keenness, alertness and a 'ready-to-go' temperament. Its ancestors were described as long ago as the seventeenth century, but not until a couple of centuries later did it exist in colours other than black and brown. At the beginning of this century, when it began to grow in numbers and for a time became one of the most popular breeds in the world, it was subjected to intensive breed improvement.

The wire fox terrier is square-built, energetic and keen. The coat is very wiry with abundant whiskers and leg hair.

White predominates, but otherwise colour is of little importance. Dogs stand just over 15in at the shoulder with a weight of about 18lb; bitches are proportionately smaller and lighter.

Ireland

209 Glen of Imaal Terrier

The Glen of Imaal terrier was not officially recognised by the Irish Kennel Club until 1933, although the breed had been used for badger and otter hunting for centuries, primarily in County Wicklow where it is considered to have originated. It is mentioned in hunting lore as early as the sixteenth century.

As a dog bred to 'go to ground', it is strong, courageous and, above all, quiet; it is still used for work rather than kept as a pet.

The Glen of Imaal terrier is a strikingly heavily built, powerful little dog with short, sturdy legs which are slightly bowed in front. The head is strongly made with small, dropped ears and brown, intelligent eyes. The tail is docked and carried smartly upwards. The coat is fairly long and very coarse.

Accepted colours are bluish grey with or without tan, and wheaten. Height at shoulder must not exceed 14in and bitches are always smaller.

210 Irish Terrier

Reputed characteristics of the Irish are, among others, red hair and a fiery temper. The first one, in particular, also characterises the Irish terrier. It represents an old type of dog which has been only recently remodelled into a modern 'breed'. Without quite achieving the impressive height of the Airedale terrier, it is one of the taller terrier breeds. In spite of its more convenient size and balanced temperament it has never quite caught on either as a pet or as a show dog.

The Irish terrier is active, lively, wiry and built for speed; it therefore has a more racy outline than most other terriers. The head is long and fairly narrow and should not fall away towards the nose. The eyes are dark and fiery. The tail is docked slightly longer than in most other terriers and is carried erect, not over the back. The coat is wiry and close but not so long as to hide the outline of the body.

The Irish terrier is whole-coloured, the most desirable colour being shades of red. Height at shoulder is about 18in, with weight around 26lb.

211 Japanese Terrier

It is debatable whether this dog should be classed as a terrier. It is undoubtedly descended from the more common British terrier breeds, mainly the smooth fox terrier, but in the course of time it has lost so much of the terrier character that one includes it in the terrier group with reluctance.

In conformation, it is most closely described as a fox terrier with a sparse, smooth coat, but it is lighter throughout and lacks, in particular, the heavy bone, short strong body and clean-cut reach of the smooth fox terrier. The colour is usually that of a fox terrier—white with smaller markings in black and tan. It is slightly higher at the shoulder than the fox terrier.

212 Kerry Blue Terrier

Of all the breeds from Ireland, there is hardly one that the Irish themselves value as highly as the Kerry blue terrier—possibly because all the other breeds have been adopted, remodelled and/or modernised by enterprising Britons.

In all basic essentials, the Kerry blue terrier is exclusively an Irish creation and did not appear outside its home country until 1920. Since then it has become popular in Britain and the USA.

How the Irish set about producing the Kerry blue is not known with certainty, but one assumes that there is a little wolfhound and a little gundog blood and quite a lot of the old hunt terrier. The breed today exhibits one of the most striking outlines to be seen in the show ring: it is compact and muscular with a profuse and soft coat.

Puppies and young dogs are always black and all too frequently the desired blue colour never appears, even in fully-grown animals. Height at shoulder for dogs is 18–19in, slightly less for bitches. The ideal weight is around 35lb.

Great Britain

213 Lakeland Terrier

The Lakeland terrier is one of the more recent terrier breeds; even though its ancestors, like those of most other terrier breeds, existed in Britain for centuries, this new variety was not called by its present name until the period between the two World Wars.

Like other small terriers, the Lakeland was originally bred exclusively for work, with no consideration for good looks. For a long time type was fairly indeterminate and for a period leaned more towards the wire fox terrier than is considered desirable today.

To the layman, the Lakeland terrier may easily be mistaken for the Welsh terrier, although it is more heavily built, usually has more coat on the head and the legs and has a greater variety of colours. According to the breed standard, the Lakeland terrier is a lively, fearless and hardworking dog.

The head is well-balanced, without being weighty, with powerful jaws. The eyes are larger than the fox terrier's and the back only moderately short. The tail, as with most terriers, is set and carried high. The coat is rough.

The colour varies from whole-coloured wheaten to pure black. Height at shoulder should not exceed just over 14in. Weight is usually around 16lb.

214 Manchester Terrier

Despite its smooth coat, the Manchester terrier is a thorough-bred terrier —albeit a fairly rare one nowadays. It resembles the smooth fox terrier (207) with which it has a great deal in common as far as origin is concerned.

The two breeds are of roughly the same age, but the Manchester terrier was crossed with sighthounds at an early stage, which made it much more graceful as well as quieter than most terriers. According to the breed standard, the Manchester terrier is a compact dog with good bone. The head is long and narrow, the eyes are small, set close, dark and sparkling. The neck is long and slightly arched, the back moderately curved and the tail, which is carried low, is thick at the root and tapers to a point. The coat is short, smooth and glossy.

The colour is jet black with clearly defined mahogany tan markings. Height at shoulder is about 16in for dogs, 15in for bitches. Weight is around 17lb.

215 Norfolk Terrier

The Norfolk terrier is probably one of the most 'modern' breeds—not until 1964 did the Kennel Club officially recognise it as a separate breed. However, it is not in any way a new breed—until 1964 it was counted as a variety of the Norwich terrier and competed in the same classes at dog shows. But whether regarded as a variety of Norwich terrier or a Norfolk in its own right, the breed has remained very popular in Britain and well supported in other countries.

In conformation, the Norfolk terrier differs from the Norwich only in a few points: its slightly longer body gives the impression of a lower profile and the ears, instead of being stiffly erect, are soft and dropped. In other respects, the Norwich terrier breed standard applies.

216 Norwich Terrier

As a breed, the Norwich terrier is very recent—it was officially recognised by the Kennel Club in 1932. It has become extremely popular in Britain and in some other countries. The breed was created by crossing the Irish terrier (210) with various short-legged terrier varieties. Like many of the British terriers, the Norwich takes its name from its place of origin and was also originally used for 'going to ground'.

The Norwich terrier is a hardy, active little dog, higher on the leg and lighter than, for example, the Scottish terrier (217). The head is not very long, but has a marked stop, a very bright and keen expression and stiffly erect ears. The body is short and compact and the tail is docked.

The colour is red, red wheaten, black and tan or grizzle. Height at shoulder is about 10in.

Great Britain
217 Scottish Terrier

The Scottish terrier has long stood as a symbol for Scotland. Though it has never reached the heights of popularity which the wire fox terrier once enjoyed, it has always had a large and constant following throughout the world. This particular breed, out of all the terrier varieties existing in northern England and Scotland before the turn of the century, came to be regarded as the truly Scottish representative as a result of propaganda. All the various Scottish breeds have about the same claim to be called Scottish, but it was the fanciers of the breed now known as the Scottish terrier who were the most persistent and managed to make their breed dominant.

The Scottish terrier is a very sturdy, thick-set dog. Despite its small size, it is very active and surprisingly agile. The head is very long with a large, black nose and deeply set, expressive eyes under the bushy eyebrows. The coat is very coarse, thick and wiry.

The colour ranges from black, wheaten or brindle. Height at shoulder is 10–11in, weight 19–23lb.

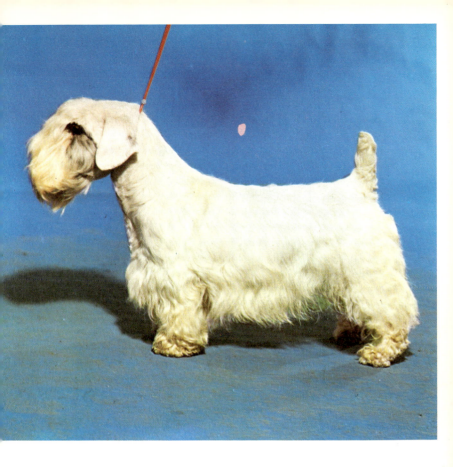

218 Sealyham Terrier

The Sealyham terrier now leads a fairly obscure existence in most parts of the world; with its sturdy appearance and go-ahead spirit it deserves greater popularity. It is another excellent example of how man is able to develop living creatures for his own purposes.

In the mid-nineteenth century an extremely ferocious cat killer was produced in Wales through intensive breeding: the most vicious local terriers were selected, crossed with various other breeds and only the fiercest of the offspring were allowed to breed. Not until well into this century was breeding directed towards the present sealyham. Thus the even type with its still hardy and obstinate—but now kindly— temperament are of comparatively recent date.

The sealyham terrier should, foremost, be strong and energetic. Despite its small size it is very heavily built and sturdy, without appearing clumsy.

The preferred colour is white, with or without lemon or brownish markings on the head and ears. Height at shoulder should not exceed 12in. Weight for dogs is 20lb maximum, 18lb for bitches.

Great Britain

219 Skye Terrier

Although the Skye terrier is not numerous at dog shows, it is one of the best known profiles in the canine world. Its extremely long body with the long, straight coat flowing from the parting along the spine to the ground generally attracts attention.

Originally, the Skye terrier had much in common with the Scottish terrier—the first Skye terriers did, in fact, compete in the same classes as its now more common relatives. Not until 1870 was it possible to distinguish clearly the two breeds and they have since grown apart even further.

The Skye terrier is a heavily built, low-set dog with a proudly carried head. The ears are pricked or, sometimes, dropped. The back is level, despite its length, and the long tail is carried low and gracefully feathered with long hair.

The colour is blue-grey or fawn. Height at shoulder is about 10in. As a comparison, incidentally, the length from the tip of the nose to the tip of the tail is about 41in!

Great Britain

220 Soft-coated Wheaten Terrier

The soft-coated wheaten terrier comes into stark contrast to the clean-cut, flashy show breeds within the terrier group. It has overall a natural, shaggy, slightly old-fashioned look, and should not be trimmed.

The soft-coated wheaten terrier originated in Ireland and was not officially recognised as a breed until 1943. It is still rare in Britain and elsewhere; even at Crufts, the largest dog show in the world, the breed usually musters no more than half a dozen entries. It is considered to be very affectionate and hardy.

The soft-coated wheaten terrier is a strong, active and spirited dog, compact in body and without exaggerated features. The head is moderately long with small, well fringed, thin ears folded forwards. The eyes are dark with an intelligent expression and the whole body is covered with a profuse, soft coat—wavy or with large, loose curls.

The colour is usually a light wheaten. Height at shoulder is about 18in and weight around 40lb.

221 Staffordshire Bull Terrier

The Staffordshire bull terrier is not one of the most popular terrier breeds, although it has a large following in its home country, Britain, and in the USA. It was not recognised as a breed by the Kennel Club until 1935. Long before it was given official status, however, it was in common use as a guard and fighting dog, though for a long time the type was very uneven.

The Staffordshire bull terrier greatly resembles the bull terrier (200), although lacking its sweeping lines and striking head shape. It is a medium-sized, fairly long-legged terrier, heavily built and thick-set. The head is broad with a marked stop and half-pricked or 'rose' ears. The coat is smooth and glossy.

The colour ranges from particolour to brindle or whole-colour in a variety of shades. Height at shoulder is 14–16in.

Tibet

222 Tibetan Terrier

One may well ask how the Tibetan terrier got its name: it certainly comes from Tibet, but it is unlikely that it possesses any terrier blood even though it has the terrier's typical lively and alert temperament.

In the rugged mountain terrain of its home country, it was originally used mainly as a herder; moreover, its profuse coat is reputed to have been shorn for wool! It is quite a newcomer to Europe—the first dogs arrived in Britain about 1930—but it has quickly gained a following.

The Tibetan terrier is alert, intelligent and game, preferably a little restrained with strangers but certainly not timid. The head has a marked stop, a black nose, large dark eyes and v-shaped pendant ears. The coat, which is profuse and either straight or wavy, is particularly abundant on the head.

The colour is usually white, grey, cream or black, but may vary considerably. Height at shoulder is 14–16in, slightly less for bitches.

223 Welsh Terrier

Originally, the Welsh terrier was as much English as it was Welsh. But while the English quarrelled about minor points in their black and tan terriers, their variety became extinct. In the meantime the Welsh breeders, who had been working to produce an even, coherent strain, managed to get 'their' dog recognised as the real type—and with their own name to boot! At one time the Welsh terrier was a coarse and unrefined hunt terrier, but once the breed was officially recognised at the beginning of this century it quickly improved and planned breeding was carried further than in most other terrier breeds.

It is not only the colour which separates the Welsh terrier from the wire fox terrier (208)—it is also more robustly built overall. It is a spirited, fearless little dog with bold bearing. The coat is coarse and wiry and the colour preferably black and tan.

Height at shoulder should not exceed just over 15in. The average weight is 20–21lb.

224 West Highland White Terrier

The West Highland white terrier, commonly known as the Westie, is now climbing very quickly towards the heights of popularity. With its appealing expression and its irrepressible temperament it has gained numerous admirers. The fact that it has a calmer disposition than most other terriers may have contributed to its success.

In the days when utilitarian factors were paramount in dog rearing, the odd all-white puppies born to the old type hunt terriers were put down as useless for hunting purposes. In time, however, a white equivalent to the Scottish terrier was wanted and after some experimental breeding a white Scottish terrier was recognised in 1905 as an official breed under the name of West Highland white terrier.

Since then, the Westie and the Scottie have gradually drifted apart in type: both are short and compact in body, but the Westie is not as extremely low-set as the Scottie. The head is not as long and is carried very high. Because of the profuse coat, the head appears almost completely round. The ears are small, pointed and carried stiffly erect and the eyes are slightly sunk into the head; they should be as dark as possible. The coat is profuse, about 2in long, and straight and hard except on the ears, where it is smooth and velvety.

The colour is pure white and height at shoulder about 11in.

Great Britain

225. Yorkshire Terrier

Within most groups of breeds there is usually a toy variety which, with the exception of size, has maintained the special characteristics of the larger breeds. A good example of this is undoubtedly the Yorkshire terrier, despite the fact that modern breeders have furnished it with a flowing coat. Its temperament, too, is typical of the terrier: it is lively, fiery and inexhaustible.

As a recognised breed, the Yorkshire terrier is of fairly recent origin; it evolved during the nineteenth century through deliberate attempts to create a new toy dog. Exactly how the British breeders concentrating on this achieved their objective is not known.

At one time the size of the dog and the length of its coat were considered of prime importance but now, fortunately, emphasis is also placed on soundness and a bright temperament. The coat should be long enough to reach the ground—which may present difficulties, overcome only by keeping the coat protected by plastic bags or tied up in 'curlers'.

The steel blue colour of the body coat should be pure and not intermingled with the tan markings on the head, chest and legs. Weight should not exceed 7lb while height at shoulder is about 8in.

Belgium

226 Tervueren (Belgian Shepherd Dog)
(Tervueren)

Like the Groenendael (71), to which it is closely related, the Tervueren resembles a light, rangy Alsatian (47), although there is little trace of Alsatian in its pedigree. Around the turn of the century there existed in Belgium—where the Tervueren and the Groenendael originated—a black sheepdog which, mated to a similarly black sheepdog bitch, produced the breed we now know as the Groenendael.

Previously, however, the same dog had been mated to another bitch—which was brown with black shadings—and the resulting litter became the ancestors of the Tervueren. The breed differs from the Groenendael chiefly in colour— brown with black tips to the coat. Height at shoulder is 24–26in for dogs, 22–25in for bitches.

Both breeds, which are fairly rare outside their home country, take their names from the Belgian villages from which they are thought to have originated: Tervueren and Groenendael near Brussels.

227 Tosa

The Japanese fighting dog, the tosa, is of comparatively recent origin: it was bred during the second half of the nineteenth century solely for arranged dog fights. The Japanese imported European breeds like bulldogs, bull terriers, St Bernards and great Danes and succeeded, as one would expect, in producing an almost invincible fighter. Although now officially prohibited in Japan, dog fights are still held illegally; however, the tosa is nowadays also employed as a guard and kept as a pet. Not surprisingly, in view of its history, the tosa has a markedly suspicious attitude towards strangers.

In conformation, the tosa resembles the mastiff: it is tall, imposing and powerfully built. The large head has amber-coloured, fairly small eyes and small, highly set, dropped ears. The tail is set high and reaches the hock. The coat is short, smooth and hard.

The colour is a reddish brown, sometimes white with red patches or reddish brown with red markings in various shades. Height at shoulder is at least 24in for dogs and at least 21in for bitches.

Sweden

228 Västgötaspitz

Should Sweden choose a breed as its national symbol, there could be no more suitable choice than the västgötaspitz. It is said to have existed since time immemorial throughout the south and midlands of Sweden. It has, moreover, had a dramatic history in modern times. Not until the 1940s was it realised that only a few of the 'Swedish herder' still existed and an intense rescue operation was launched. This resulted in a quick consolidation of type and a fairly rapid growth in numbers, at least in Sweden.

The västgötaspitz is a short-legged, active and alert little spitz. It is generally lighter than the Welsh corgi (233), the back is not as long and the legs not quite as short. The tail is short—the västgötaspitz is often born with a bobbed tail. The coat is hard, fairly short and close.

The colour varies from wolf grey to red fawn with darker shadings on the back and lighter shadings on the underside of the body. Sparse white markings are acceptable. Height at shoulder is 13–16in.

Hungary

229 Hungarian Vizsla, Short-haired
(Vizsla)

The Hungarian vizsla is said to be equally suitable as a family
dog or gundog. In recent years it has become quite popular
as a show dog in many countries, but in its home country
it is more frequently used as a gundog. Its resemblance to
the pointer (127) and the German short-haired pointer (49)
is evident but not striking.

The main characteristic of the vizsla is probably its colour,
which is a 'rusty gold'. Characteristic, too, is the pale liver-
coloured nose; the colour of the eyes harmonises with the
colour of the coat, but should not be yellow. In general conformation the vizsla is more robust and less refined than the
pointer, its head is coarser with larger ears and the tail is
docked. In temperament, it is lively, affectionate and easy
to train. There are two types of coat, short-haired and wire-
haired.

Apart from rusty gold, the colour may also be a sandy
yellow in varying shades. Height at shoulder is 22–24in for
dogs, 21–23in for bitches.

230 Hungarian Vizsla, Wire-haired
(Vizsla, Drotszoruvizsla)

It is believed that the wire-haired vizsla came into existence
through a mutation in the more common short-haired variety.
Subsequently, it was successfully crossed with the German
wire-haired pointer; because of its coat, the wire-haired vizsla
seems heavier and less elegant than its short-haired relative.
The eyes are a shade darker in colour than the coat, but
should be neither black nor yellow. The coat is thick, wiry
and fairly long except on the head which, apart from bushy
eyebrows and whiskers, is smooth-haired. The colour of the
coat is fawn without markings.

Height at shoulder for dogs is 22–25in, 21–24in for bitches.
Weight varies between 48–66lb.

231 Wachtelhund

The spaniel is almost exclusively a British 'invention'—the wachtelhund is one of the few European counterparts with any claim to fame. It is mainly employed as a water retriever but in its home country is also used for tracking game or driving it to the guns. It originated in Germany, but was threatened with extinction by imported British spaniels who showed that they could work as efficiently in Germany as in Britain. A few German breeders rescued the breed and gained official recognition for it at the turn of the century.

The wachtelhund most closely resembles the English springer spaniel (171), but it does not have the springer's typical spaniel head; the muzzle is not as deep and square and the ears are not as big. The coat is more profuse overall and is wavy—more abundant on the ears, neck, chest, underside of the body, at the back of the forelegs and on the thighs.

The colour is usually liver. Height at shoulder is 18–20in for dogs, 16–18in for bitches.

232 Weimaraner   *Germany*

Although the small German gundog group is dominated by the German pointer—the short-haired and wire-haired—it is the Weimaraner which is the oldest type. It is said to have been systematically bred at the court in Weimar towards the end of the eighteenth century and the type has been kept fairly pure ever since. It has, however, never become very popular, though in recent years it has become an exclusive show dog in Britain and America.

The Weimaraner is a powerful, elegant dog with a proudly carried head, which in many ways resembles the pointer's. The bridge of the nose, however, is convex rather than concave and the Weimaraner also has larger ears than the pointer; they are set high and are supple and lobular. The body is well developed and muscular, the legs well boned and the hindquarters well angulated.

There are short-haired, wire-haired and long-haired Weimaraners, but the short-haired variety is probably the most common. The tail of the two former varieties is docked two thirds from the the root, while only the tip of the tail in the long-haired Weimaraner is removed.

The colour is shades of grey, usually a very special silver grey colour which is rare in other breeds. Height at shoulder is 23–25in for dogs, 22–24in for bitches.

233 Welsh Corgi, Cardigan

When talking of the Welsh corgi one usually refers to the Pembroke (234), which is the more common of the two varieties of Welsh corgi. The other, the Cardigan corgi, is very rare outside Britain and even in its home country may be represented by only a few animals at dog shows.

The Cardigan corgi is slightly larger and heavier overall than the Pembroke corgi and is usually considered to be calmer and quieter in temperament. The tail is long and shaped like a sabre. The head has a more sharp and watchful expression than the Pembroke corgi's and the ears are larger and more rounded.

All colours except pure white are acceptable, but red or brindle with white markings, or blue merle, are most popular. Height at shoulder is about 12in.

234 Welsh Corgi, Pembroke

The bob-tailed Pembroke corgi is probably the spitz breed with the greatest claim to international fame. As the special favourite of the British Royal Family it has got plenty of publicity and has quickly spread to most parts of the world. Pretty good progress for a little Celtic cattle dog!

The Welsh corgi is the only British spitz breed—but one wonders whether it was originally a Scandinavian breed. Its resemblance to the Swedish västgötaspitz (228) is too striking to ignore. Although both breeds represent a very old type of spitz, it was a long time before they were recognised by the kennel clubs of their respective countries—the Welsh corgi was first exhibited at a dog show in Britain in 1928.

The Pembroke Welsh Corgi is a low-set dog, slightly fox-like in appearance and with bold bearing. The head is carried proudly and the corgi has an alert and intelligent expression. The ears are fairly large and pricked. The body is rather long with a level back and short, heavily boned, straight legs. The tail is usually short by nature. The coat is thick, but not coarse.

The colour ranges from self red to tricolour with white markings on legs, neck and muzzle. Height at shoulder is 10–12in, weight around 22lb.

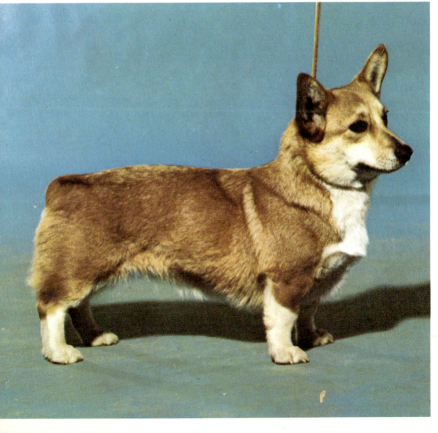

235 Wetterhoun

The Wetterhoun is probably the only Dutch gundog which has spread, albeit on a modest scale, outside its home country. Although also known as the Dutch spaniel it has little in common with the British spaniel breeds either in looks or temperament: in conformation it resembles a larger and heavier Stabyhoun (179) with some similarity to the Newfoundland (105). It is regarded as keen in temperament and thus excellent as a guard dog.

The eyes are dark or light chestnut brown, depending on the colour of the coat. The ears are dropped, with the unusual characteristic of fairly long, wavy hair at the base which gradually becomes shorter and smoother towards the tip. The tail is spiral-shaped.

The colour is black, brown and white or blue and white. Height at shoulder for dogs is about 22in and about an inch less for bitches.

236 Whippet

The origin of the whippet is obscure, but it is believed that it evolved in Britain during the past three centuries. It probably descends from small greyhounds and various types of terrier and was even used early in its history for racing and rabbiting. In some whippets the lively terrier blood is still apparent while others have the quiet disposition typical of the sighthound. It would be difficult to find a more easily manageable and attractive house dog and companion.

In conformation, the whippet is a smaller copy of the greyhound (64), though with a slightly sturdier frame. The head is long and lean, the jaws powerful and the eyes dark. The ears are fine in texture, with the tips folded when the dog is alert. The back is slightly arched over the loin with well defined flanks. It gives a general impression of beautifully balanced muscular power combined with great elegance. It should not appear light or weedy.

Fawn, brindle and white in various combinations are the most common colours, but any colour or mixture of colours is acceptable. Height at shoulder is just over 18in for dogs and about 17in for bitches.

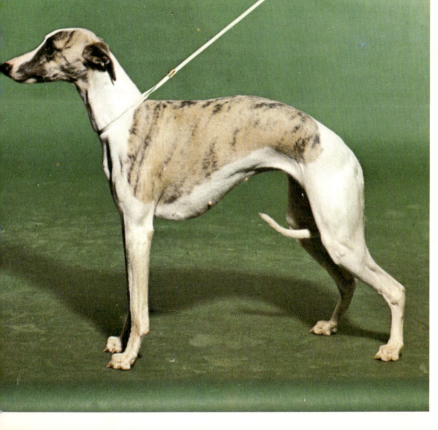

Less common breeds and varieties

As in the previous section, the breeds are listed in alphabetical order and numbered. These numbers are also used in the index and for reference purposes in the text matter.

USA
237 American Foxhound

The main difference between the American foxhound and its English ancestor breed (58) is size: although the British do not place undue emphasis on size, and great variations may occur, the English foxhound hardly ever approaches the American foxhound in stature. The two breeds were originally used for similar purposes, but while the foxhound in Britain is never shown at ordinary dog shows, the American foxhound is now comparatively popular as a show dog in its home country.

In conformation, the American foxhound is an imposing, upstanding, long-legged dog and generally gives a rangier impression than its English counterpart. The ears are large and dropped and the eyes have an appealing expression. The body is strong and well built with very well boned legs, and the tail, carried straight up, is sparsely coated on the underside with long, coarse hair.

All colours are acceptable. Height at shoulder is usually just over 24in.

Yugoslavia
238 Balkanski Gonic

This Balkan harrier/foxhound type breed is heavily built and rectangular in shape. The head is long with chestnut brown, clear eyes and rounded, dropped ears. The fairly short tail is thick at the root and may be either straight or slightly curved. The coat is short, thick and coarse. The predominant colour is red or chestnut brown with a black saddle.

Height at shoulder is 18–21in for dogs, 17–20in for bitches. Weight is around 44lb.

France
239 Barbet

The barbet is not very common today, but it is of ancient origin and is a forebear of many modern breeds, ranging from the poodle (31) to the German pointer (49). It roughly resembles a mixture of those breeds: a shaggy and not very refined type of dog. It is considered to be excellent for working in water.

Breed points of the barbet include a deep chest and an arched loin, a short, broad muzzle and low-set, dropped ears. The tail, too, is low-set but is carried high, sometimes curled at the end. The feet are large and broad and the action is markedly stilted. The coat is woolly, long and thick and has a shaggy look.

The colour may be white with black markings, dark grey, fawn or off-white with brown markings. Height at shoulder is 18–22in.

Yugoslavia
240 Basanski Ostrodlaki Gonic-Barak

This tracking hound from Bosnia has a fairly long and profuse coat all over. The eyes are large, oval in shape and chestnut brown. The ears are set high, rounded at the tips and hanging. The tail is long and well covered with hair.

Height at shoulder and weight may vary considerably, but about 21in and 44lb respectively are ideal.

France
241 Berger des Pyrenées à Face Rasée

This breed is practically identical with the berger des Pyrenées (15) apart from the coat, which is short

237 American Foxhound

242 Bichon à Poil Frisé

239 Barbet

243 Bichon Havanais

**240 Basanski Ostrodlaki
Gonic-Barak**

244 Billy

**241 Berger des Pyrenées à
Face Rasée**

**245 Bleu de Gascogne,
Basset**

and fine on the head (though not on the rest of the body).

The colour of this 'clean shaven' variety may extend to piebald or brindle. It may also be slightly taller, but height at shoulder for dogs is usually 16–18in, 16–17in for bitches.

242 Bichon à Poil Frisé

Under the somewhat simplified names of 'bichon frisé' or 'bichon', this breed has in recent years enjoyed a vast upsurge in popularity, especially in the USA. It lies midway in type between the poodles (33) and the Maltese (99). Its history is similar to that of other toy breeds from the Mediterranean area; it was a prized pet for women in the higher social classes in medieval times. The coat is very profuse, especially on the head, and is slightly curly and silky in texture.

The colour is white, or white with café-au-lait or dark grey patches on the ears and the body. Height at shoulder should not exceed 12in, preferably considerably less.

Cuba
243 Bichon Havanais

The International Canine Federation, the FCI, does not indicate a country of origin for the bichon Havanais, despite the fact that its name implies Cuban connections. Although its ancestors came from Italy and France, it is probably beyond dispute that the breed existed in Cuba several centuries ago.

The bichon Havanais is slightly more rectangular in build than its close relatives, the Maltese (99) and the bichon à poil frisé (242). It has a broad skull, but a fairly pointed foreface, very dark eyes and dropped ears folded forwards. The tail is carried in a plume over the back. The coat is long and silky, slightly wavy at the tips and may vary in colour from white and fawn to tobacco brown. It is sometimes particoloured.

There is no height at shoulder specified for the breed, but weight should not exceed 13lb.

France
244 Billy

The Billy is a French breed which evolved during the nineteenth century and was bred specifically for hunting deer and wild boar. The Poitevin (299), as well as lesser known French breeds, figure in the pedigree. The breed takes its name from the town of Billy in Haut-Poitou.

It is a tall and elegant dog with a long, fairly narrow head. The ears are set low and hang down, the tail is long and carried low. The coat is short, but fairly coarse in texture. The colour is always white or cream, occasionally with orange patches or an orange saddle.

Height at shoulder is 24–26in for dogs, 23–25in for bitches.

France
245 Bleu de Gascogne, Basset

The basset bleu de Gascogne is not only smaller than other closely related varieties, it also differs in its usually crooked legs. Its body shape is distinctly rectangular and height at shoulder should not exceed 12–15in.

France
246 Bleu de Gascogne, Petit

The main difference between the grand bleu de Gascogne and this, the small blue tracking dog from Gascogne lies, apart from size, in its job of work: the smaller variety is generally used for hunting the hare. In most other respects, the same breed standard applies, except that the petit bleu de Gascogne should not exceed 19–22in at the shoulder.

France
247 Bleu de Gascogne, Petit Griffon

This, the wire-haired variety of the blue de Gascogne family, is similar in some ways to the more common griffon varieties (67–70). It is extremely rare, has slightly smaller ears than its 'blue' relatives and measures 17–21in at the shoulder.

248 Bolognese

The Bolognese resembles a 'silky poodle' or a long-legged Maltese (99). The breed is closely related to the other toy breeds from the Mediterranean area—the bichon varieties, for example—and is believed to originate from Bologna, where it existed in medieval times.

The Bolognese has large, dark eyes, dropped ears and a tail set high and carried curled over the back. The coat is profuse and long, silky in texture and extends from the nose to the tip of the tail. The colour is pure white. Fawn markings are not desirable. Height at shoulder for dogs is 11–12in, 10–11in for bitches.

249 Bouvier des Ardennes

There are two varieties of the sturdy bouvier des Ardennes—the larger and the smaller—and, in its country of origin, is nearly as popular as the better known variety from Flanders (21). It is said to be still employed in its original role as a swine herding dog in some parts of the country. It is also reputed to be hostile to strangers but very affectionate to its master.

The head is large and heavy with bushy whiskers, beard and eyebrows. The ears are not cropped and are carried stiffly erect, although semi-erect ears are acceptable. The tail is docked very short. The coat is coarse in texture, but not long. The hair on the legs and feet is short.

All colours are acceptable. Height at shoulder should not exceed 24in for the smaller variety; the larger variety should be over 24in.

250 Braque d'Ariège

This smooth-haired braque originates from the southern parts of France. It resembles the German short-haired pointer (49) or the pointer (127), but is not as clean-cut in outline. The nose may be flesh coloured or chestnut brown, the eyes are not necessarily dark. The ears are carried close to the head and the tail is docked to half its natural length. The short coat is predominantly white, with uneven patches of orange or chestnut brown.

Height at shoulder is 24–26in.

251 Braque du Bourbonnais

The braque variety from Bourbonnais is sometimes referred to simply as the 'short-tailed braque' because of its characteristically short tail. Another special feature of this breed is its colour: white with small chestnut brown spots evenly distributed all over the body. Height at shoulder is usually about 22in.

252 Braque Dupuy

This dog takes its name from Pierre Dupuy, a Frenchman who is thought to have been the first to breed braques of this variety at the beginning of this century. The braque Dupuy is very graceful and has something of the distinctive look of the long-legged sighthounds. The general impression is that of power combined with elegance. The head is longer and more narrow than in most other braque varieties, the ears are fairly small, supple and pendulous. The eyes are golden brown or brown in colour. The long and thin tail is carried low and is slightly curved sabre-fashion. The coat is smooth, fairly short and is white with dark chestnut-coloured patches.

Height at shoulder is about 27in for dogs and about 26in for bitches.

253 Braque Français de Petite Taille

The smaller of the French braque varieties has evolved over a long period of careful breeding aimed at reducing its size without losing its excellent abilities as a gundog. It is now used mainly in south-western France and differs from the larger braque Français (25) by, among other things, its shorter and smoother coat.

Height at shoulder is 19–22in, ie not exceeding the minimum height of its larger relative.

246 Bleu de Gascogne, Petit

250 Braque d'Ariège

247 Bleu de Gascogne, Petit Griffon

251 Braque du Bourbonnais

248 Bolognese

252 Braque Dupuy

249 Bouvier des Ardennes

253 Braque Français de Petite Taille

254 Câo de Agua

The Portuguese water dog was previously very common in all seaports along the coast of Portugal and Spain. It was then used exclusively as a working dog on board the boats and was invaluable as a retriever of tackle, nets, etc. Today it exists mainly in the Algarve area. It has a reputation as a formidable fighter but is good tempered and friendly with people.

In conformation the Portuguese water dog slightly resembles the poodle—possibly because of the characteristic 'lion clip'. The origin of the breed is unknown, but theories about a common ancestry for the water dog and the poodle have been put forward. Other breed points are the large head, which looks even larger because of the profuse coat; the long tail, which is curved over the back and has a tuft of hair at the tip and, particularly uncommon, the webbed feet. There are two coat varieties: long-coated and curly-coated.

The colour may be black or brown or either of these colours combined with white. It may also be grey or pure white. Ideal height at shoulder is around 21in for dogs and 18in for bitches.

255 Câo de Castro Laboreiro

This large Portuguese breed takes its name from the village of Castro Laboreiro. It is of the mastiff type, but is not as heavy as most breeds of that class; it resembles the tall, heavy Labrador retriever (138). In its home area, it is used mainly as a guard—sometimes as protection against wolves. The head is of retriever type but less refined and the ears are of medium size and carried close to the head. The eyes are chestnut brown in light-coloured dogs and almost black in dark varieties. The tail is long and thick and carried low when the dog is at rest, but straight up or over the back in action. The tail should not, however touch the back.

The colour is wolf grey in light or dark shades. Height at shoulder is 22–24in for dogs, 20–22in for bitches. Weight is around 66–88lb and 44–66lb respectively.

256 Câo da Serra da Estrela

The Portuguese sheepdog is now well distributed all over Portugal, but it is still considered that the best types come from the slopes of the Estrela mountains. The breed is large and heavy and valued as a housedog as well as a guard for livestock. Its affinity to the mastiff type is apparent—especially the body shape—although the head is lighter and less blunt in the foreface. The eyes are dark amber and the ears small, triangular and dropped. The neck is short and thick, the body sturdily built and the tail long and sabre-shaped. The colour may be shades of wolf grey or fawn, whole-coloured or particoloured.

Height at shoulder ranges from 26–28in for dogs, 24–27in for bitches. A fully mature dog often weighs up to 110lb.

257 Câo de Serra de Aires

In the mountainous country of its native land, this breed herds cattle, pigs and horses. It is rectangular in shape with a large and broad head and round, preferably dark, eyes. The ears are triangular and pendant and the tail is long and slightly curved. The coat is long, soft and moderately wavy. The breed bears a close resemblance to the better known bearded collie (41).

Height at shoulder for dogs is 17–19in, 16–18in for bitches. Weight is around 26–40lb.

258 Chien d'Artois

The French hound, the chien d'Artois, resembles either a long-legged basset hound (10) or a light bloodhound (18). The head is less extreme than in the basset or the bloodhound but it is of a roughly similar type with long, low-set ears. The tail is long and carried high and the coat is short and smooth. The colour is tricolour.

Height at shoulder is about 20–23in.

254 Cào de Agua

258 Chien d'Artois

255 Cào de Castro Laboreiro

259 Chien Français Blanc et Noir

256 Cào da Serra da Estrela

260 Chien Français Blanc et Orange

257 Cào de Serra de Aires

261 Chien Français Tricolore

262 Cirneco dell'Etna

266 Deutscher Stichelhaar-iger Vorstehhund

263 Dachsbracke

267 Ellinikós Ichnilátis

264 Westfälischer Dachsbracke

269 Epagneul Picard

265 Deutscher Langhaariger Vorstehhund

270 Erdelyi Kopo

France
259 Chien Français Blanc et Noir

This French hound—which in 1957 was divided into three varieties according to size and colour—is a local equivalent to the internationally better known foxhound (58). The black-and-white variety is slightly larger than the orange-and-white and tricolour varieties and, compared to the foxhound, has a slightly domed skull and a longer, narrower head. The tail is considerably thinner and neater. The colour is white with large black markings on the head and back and smaller roan markings on the rest of the body. Above the eyes and, occasionally, on the cheeks, there may be a fawn spot.

Height at shoulder is 26–28in for dogs, 25–27in for bitches.

France
260 Chien Français Blanc et Orange

The white-and-orange coloured French hound is basically a descendant of the Poitevin and the Billy, but at dog shows it is judged by the same standard as the chien Français tricolore—except, of course, on colour, which is white with orange patches on the head and body.

France
261 Chien Français Tricolore

The tricolour French hound has the same background as the black-and-white variety: a combination of old French hounds and imported British blood.

Roughly the same breed standard applies to the two breeds, but the tricolour has chestnut-colored eyes instead of dark brown and, of course, differs in colour—a combination of black, white and tan.

Height at shoulder may be an inch or so lower than in the black-and-white variety—about 24–27in.

Italy
262 Cirneco dell'Etna

The cirneco dell'Etna is one of the smaller sighthound breeds and, in common with most of its relatives within the group, is thought to be very old. It probably moved from Egypt to Sicily well over a thousand years ago but, as distinct from its nearest relatives, the Ibizan hound (126) and the Pharaoh hound (121), it remains quite unknown outside Italy.

It resembles a small, light greyhound (64) with the style of a crop-eared Dobermann (50): the ears are long and pointed. It is not as deep in chest, nor as well angulated and muscular as the greyhound. The eyes are amber in colour and the nose flesh-coloured. The coat is very short and fine on the head and ears, slightly longer and silky in texture on the rest of the body. The colour is whole-coloured in any shade of fawn, but small white markings are acceptable. Pure white or white with orange markings is also acceptable.

Height at shoulder for dogs is about 18–20in and 17–18in for bitches. Weight is around 26–30lb and 22–26lb respectively.

Germany
263 Dachsbracke

The dachsbracke's blood relationship to the dachshund is apparent: to the layman it could easily be mistaken for a heavier, more long-legged and coarser version of the smooth dachshund (189). In its home country it is used for tracking and locating its prey by scent—especially in difficult and rugged terrain where its slow and deliberate progress in working out the line of scent is a great asset. There are several colour varieties: black with tan markings, different shades of tan, or white with tan markings.

Height at shoulder is 13–17in.

Germany
264 Westfälischer Dachsbracke

The Westphalian dachsbracke is much smaller than its cousin (263). Its resemblance to the Swedish drever (53) is apparent and reflects the close relationship. The colour is usually a reddish-fawn with white markings, sometimes extensive. Black and chocolate brown are considered less desirable.

Height at shoulder is 12–14in.

Germany
265 Deutscher Langhaariger Vorstehhund

The German long-haired pointer is much rarer than the short-haired and the wire-haired varieties. It differs in type by its softer, more setter-like outline and resembles a fairly coarse Irish setter (158) or a drentse patrijshond (52). The eyes should be as dark as possible. The coat on the body is about 2in in length, but longer on the neck, chest, thighs and underside of the body. The legs and the tail are well feathered. The tail need not be docked.

The colour is liver or white with liver markings. The long-haired variety may be quite a bit taller than other German pointers: it is usually over 25in and may stand up to 28in at the shoulder.

Germany
266 Deutscher Stichelhaariger Vorstehhund

The main difference between this variety of German pointer and the German wire-haired pointer (48) is its coat, which is more profuse and longer. It is, however, very coarse. The eyes are usually light brown but may vary according to the colour of the coat, as long as they are not yellow. The tail is usually docked to half its length. The coat colour is liver brown with white markings.

Height at shoulder is about 24–26in for dogs, slightly less for bitches.

Greece
267 Ellinikós Ichnilátis

The Hellenic hound is a versatile hunter: it can track or drive in mountainous terrain as well as it does on the plains, and will hunt on its own or in packs. It is considered to have a very sonorous, deep voice.

It is of medium size and is generally slightly less powerfully built than its northern hound relatives. The head is long, the eyes chestnut brown, the nose black and the ears carried close to the head. In body shape it is rectangular and the long back is slightly arched. The tail is not very long, is fairly highly set and carried curved sabre-fashion. The coat is short, close and rather hard to the touch. It should be black with brown markings (black and tan), possibly with a small white spot on the chest. Height at shoulder is 19–22in for dogs, 18–21in for bitches. Weight is around 37–44lb.

France
268 Epagneul Bleu de Picardie

The blue spaniel from Picardy is just another colour variety of the epagneul Picard described in the following breed notes. Instead of the Picard's tan patches, it has black markings on a blue merle base colour. In other respects, the same breed standard applies for both varieties.

France
269 Epagneul Picard

The French spaniel from Picardy is widely used as a gundog in the marshlands of northern France. It was established in the nineteenth century and competed at the earliest French dog shows. In conformation it differs from British spaniels, being lighter and leggier—something like a cross between an English springer spaniel and an English setter (171 and 156).

In common with its closer relatives among the French spaniels, the epagneul Picard has a brown nose and dark amber-coloured eyes. The ears are set much higher than in most other spaniels. The moderately long tail, which is not docked, forms an elongated 'S' shape. The coat is profuse—especially on the ears, chest and tail—and slightly wavy at the tips. The hair on the head is slightly softer and finer than on the body.

The colour is a greyish blue merle with chestnut-coloured patches, especially on the head and feet. Height at shoulder is 22–24in, though the upper measure may be exceeded by about 1in in dogs.

Hungary
270 Erdelyi Kopo

This Hungarian hound originates from Transylvania and is particularly

277

noted for its obedience, trainability and exceptionally good sense of direction. There are two types: the long-legged variety is used for wild boar hunting and the smaller for hunting foxes and hares.

In conformation, the erdelyi kopo has much in common with the Central European group of foxhound/harrier type hounds. It is rectangular in shape, with dark and slightly obliquely set eyes and high-set ears carried close to the head. The tail is curved at the tip.

The larger variety of erdelyi kopo has a longer and thicker coat than its smaller relative. This larger variety is usually black, the smaller variety red. Height at shoulder is 22–26in and 18–20in respectively. Weight may vary between 66–77lb.

Canada
271 Eskimo Dog

The sled dogs from Canada and Greenland are so similar in type that it is debatable whether they should be regarded as two breeds. What applies to the Greenland dog (72) also largely applies to the Eskimo dog; generally speaking, the latter is considered to be slightly shorter in back and heavier overall, without being taller. Even this, however, cannot be claimed to be a hard and fast rule.

All colours are acceptable. Weight varies considerably (a dog may weight twice as much as a bitch—both within the standard) but it is usually between 77–88lb. No height at shoulder is specified, but normally it is around 24in.

Brazil
272 Fila Brasileiro

The Brazilian mastiff is directly descended from the Spanish mastiffs which accompanied the conquistadors on their voyages to South America in the sixteenth century. Since then it has changed, so much so that the International Canine Federation, the FCI, has recognised it as a separate Brazilian breed (see also the mastin Español, 100).

It is a typical mastiff breed: powerful and imposing with a well boned frame and a heavy head. The hindquarters appear slightly higher and lighter than the forequarters and the

tail is thick at the root and tapering towards the tip. The eyes are dark, the ears fairly large, v-shaped and hanging. The coat is short, close and soft.

The fila Brasileiro is brindle or self-coloured in any colour, but white markings are confined to the feet and the tip of the tail. It usually has a black mask and black ears. The official breed standard does not specify height, but 26–28in is the average size.

France
273 Gascon Saintongeois

The French hound Gascon Saintongeois, used for tracking game or driving it to the guns, is the product of cross-breeding carried out just over a century ago. Today, it is rare even in France and virtually non-existent elsewhere.

There are two varieties: grand and petit. The latter originates from south-west France and, with the exception of size, is identical with the larger variety. The breed is fairly similar in type to the grand bleu de Gascogne (63), but has a strikingly long head with very long, thin ears hanging in folds, set low and well back. The coat is short.

White predominates with black markings, but with brown markings on the head. A common feature is a greyish brown patch on the thigh, resembling dead leaves in colour. Height at shoulder for the larger variety is 25–28in for dogs, 24–26in for bitches. The smaller variety is about 3in below these measurements.

Belgium
274 Griffon Belge

The griffon Belge differs from the more common griffon Bruxellois (66) in one respect only: it is black and tan, with these colours intermingling all over the body. Pure black or grizzle are also acceptable.

France
275 Griffon Fauve de Bretagne

The fawn griffon from Brittany is probably very old; modern types

271 Eskimo Dog

275 Griffon Fauve de Bretagne

272 Fila Brasileiro

276 Griffon Vendéen, Briquet

273 Gascon Saintongeois

277 Harlekinpinscher

274 Griffon Belge

278 Harrier

show a striking likeness to dogs depicted in medieval times. Reputedly used for wolf hunting at one time, the breed is now rare, even in its native area.

It is of medium size, very muscular and well boned. The eyes are dark and expressive, the nose black or brown. The ears are pendulous and long enough to be capable of being extended beyond the tip of the nose. The back is short and broad. The tail is of medium length with a slight curve at the end and is carried in line with the back. The coat, which should not be long and never woolly, is exceedingly coarse.

The colour is fawn, preferably in shades of golden or reddish brown. Height at shoulder is 20–22in for dogs, 19–21in for bitches.

France
276 Griffon Vendéen, Briquet

This is a smaller variety of the grand griffon Vendéen (70). It has been generally established since about 1910 and is used in Europe mainly for tracking game or driving it to the guns.

Height at shoulder is between 20–22in for dogs and 19–21in for bitches.

Germany
277 Harlekinpinscher

The harlequin pinscher is descended from its better known relative, the pinscher (123), but differs in its smaller size and colour: it is predominantly white or light in colour with darker, sometimes brindle, even patches.

Height at shoulder is 12–14in.

Great Britain
278 Harrier

The harrier belongs to the group of hounds which hunt by scent. It takes its name from the Norman word 'harier', which means a general hunting dog. In 1750, the well known English cynologist Dr Caius divided the breed into two varieties, the staghound and the dwarf foxhound. At the end of the eighteenth century when English huntsmen took up hare hunting, the harrier was found to be

particularly well suited for this work, partly because of its size. The breed is now very rare even in Britain and is not officially recognised by the Kennel Club.

The harrier resembles a smaller version of its close relative, the foxhound (58). It is a smooth-haired dog of medium size with dropped ears and a long tail. The coat is short, hard and close. The colour is the same as the foxhound's: usually tan with a black saddle and white markings, or white with lemon markings. Height at shoulder is 19–21in.

Yugoslavia
279 Hrvatski Ovcar

The Croatian sheepdog is of distinct spitz type with an alert expression, erect, pointed ears and a cone-shaped head. It is, however, longer in body than most other spitz breeds and may be naturally tailless or docked. The coat is thick and slightly wavy on the body, profuse on the back of the thighs and around the neck but short on the head, legs and feet. The colour is black—small white markings are acceptable but not desirable.

Height at shoulder for both dogs and bitches varies from 16–20in.

Yugoslavia
280 Illyrian Hound

The Illyrian hound is a powerful and heavily built dog, used for hunting wild boar, foxes and hares. It is rectangular in outline, with a broad head, long pendulous ears and a slightly curved tail. The coat is coarse and hard. It may be white, fawn, tan or grey with smaller markings, especially on the ears, in a contrasting colour.

Height at shoulder is about 18–22in.

Yugoslavia
281 Istrski Kratkodlaki Gonic

The Istrian sporting dog bears a striking resemblance to a somewhat plain pointer (127); it is not, however, used as a pointing gundog but for locating its prey by scent and driving it to the guns. Colour, according to the breed standard, is 'snow white' with orange markings on the ears. These markings may also extend to the body, particularly at the root of the tail.

Height at shoulder for dogs varies between 18–23in, while bitches should not exceed 21in. The average weight is around 40lb.

282 Istrski Resati Gonic

The wire-haired Istrian hound shares most of the characteristics of its smooth-haired relative (281) with the exception of the coat which is straight, coarse and abundant.

Yugoslavia
283 Jugoslavenski Drobojni Gonic

The tricolour Yugoslavian sporting dog is a fairly small and not very heavily built hound with a rectangular body shape, dark gentle eyes and rounded ears carried close to the head. The tail is carried in line with the back and may be either straight or, to quote the breed standard, 'shaped like a Turkish sabre'. The coat is short, close and glossy. Slight feathering on the underside of the tail is acceptable. The predominant colour is black, with a fawn shade on the legs, abdomen, tail and underside of the body. The head has golden markings and a white blaze is desirable. The light markings should not dominate and are acceptable only on the head, chest, neck and feet, but not on the body.

Height at shoulder varies between 18–22in.

Yugoslavia
284 Jugoslavenski Planinski Gonic

The Yugoslavian mountain hound is of the same size as its tricolour relative (283) but is much heavier in build. The eyes are dark, the ears carried close to the head and rounded at the tips, and the tail reaches the hock. The coat is close and coarse with a thick undercoat. The basic colour is black with tan markings. A small white spot on the chest is acceptable.

Height at shoulder is 18–22in.

Yugoslavia
285 Krasky Ovcar

This Yugoslavian sheepdog from Karst is probably most like the Leonberger (93), although the krasky ovcar is much smaller and lighter. The body shape is rectangular and the ears small, v-shaped and carried close to the head. The tail is long and sabre-shaped, often curled into a ring at the end. It is carried low when the dog is at rest and in line with the back or higher when in action. The coat is profuse with a thick undercoat, and is shorter on the head, legs and feet. The colour is iron grey, possibly with a small white spot on the chest.

The ideal height at shoulder for dogs is 23in, 21in for bitches.

Japan
286 Kyushu Nippon Inu, Shika

The kyushu, to use one of its many names, is one of the medium-sized Japanese spitz breeds. Like the ainou (4), some of its predecessors come from the island of Hokkaido and the two breeds have on occasions been crossed. The kyushu, however, is usually an inch or so taller. It was at one time used for deer hunting, but today the kyushu is kept mainly as a guard and companion. It is said to be exceptionally affectionate.

The length of its back slightly exceeds its height at the shoulder. The eyes are small and triangular in shape and the tail is loosely curled over the back. It has a lively and friendly disposition.

The colour may be shades of pepper and salt, red, black or white. Height at shoulder for dogs is 19–21in, 17–19in for bitches.

France
287 Levesque

The French hound levesque is descended from a cross between the bleu de Gascogne (63) and the foxhound (58); this cross subsequently interbred with other hound varieties. The breed is barely a century old, but is considered to be fairly even in type. The eyes are light brown and the ears, set in line with the eyes, are pendulous and long but should not trail on the ground when the dog is

279 Hrvatski Ovcar

284 Jugoslavenski Planinsk: Gonic

281 Istrski Kratkodlaki Gonic

286 Kyushu Nippon Inu, Shika

282 Istrski Resati Gonic

287 Levesque

283 Jugoslavenski Drobojni Gonic

288 Mastin de los Pirineos

289 Grosser Münsterländer

293 Schweizer Niederlaufhund

290 Berner Niederlaufhund

294 Pastore Bergamasco

291 Jura Niederlaufhund

295 Perdigueiro Português

292 Luzerner Niederlaufhund

296 Perro de Pastor Catalan

tracking. The tail is long, thick at the root, set high and carried in a curve. The coat is short.

The colour is always black and white, often with a purplish tint to the black. Height at shoulder is 26–28in for dogs, 25–27in for bitches.

Spain
288 Mastin de los Pirineos

The Pyrenean mastiff should not be confused with the internationally better known Pyrenean mountain dog (34). Although the two breeds have some points in common, the former is still of distinct mastiff type. The head is broad and heavy with a rounded skull and it has small, fairly pointed dropped ears. The thick tail is carried in an upward curve, but not over the back, when the dog is moving. The coat is more profuse than in other mastiffs; it is thick and coarse with feathering on the tail and is more abundant around the neck and on the back of the thighs.

The colour is white with two large patches of grey or fawn on the head and, occasionally, on the body. Height at shoulder varies between 28–32in. Weight is 120–155lb.

Germany
289 Grosser Münsterländer

In most respects, the large Münsterländer is similar to the more common, smaller variety. Its colour, however, is usually white with black markings—either large patches or a mass of small 'freckles', commonly called roan. All-black is considered less desirable (see also small Münsterländer, 105).

Height at shoulder is 23–25in—about 4in taller than the small Münsterländer.

Switzerland
290 Berner Niederlaufhund
291 Jura Niederlaufhund
292 Luzerner Niederlaufhund
293 Schweizer Niederlaufhund

These short-legged Swiss tracking/driving dogs are smaller versions of the long-legged varieties with similar names. They have evolved through crosses between the original type and various smaller breeds, notably the dachshund (189–191), and differ from their larger relatives in the shape of the head as well as size. The niederlaufhund has a longer, lighter and leaner head than the larger Swiss laufhund. Because of the short legs, its body shape looks distinctly rectangular (see also Swiss laufhund 150).

The difference between the four varieties is colour, and each of the niederlaufhund varieties is of the same colour as its corresponding relative in the more long-legged laufhund family. Height at shoulder is only about 12–15in.

Italy
294 Pastore Bergamasco

The Italian herder, the pastore bergamasco, includes the French briard among its ancestors; its luxuriant coat resembles that of the Hungarian puli. It is squarely built with soft, pendulous ears and large eyes matching the coat in colour. The tail reaches the hock and is sabre-shaped. The coat is long and soft, curly or wavy and profuse from the nose to the tip of the tail. The colour is whole-coloured in shades of grey, ranging from off-white to near black.

Ideal height at shoulder is 24in for dogs and 22in for bitches, with an allowance of an inch or so either way. Weight is 70–84lb and 57–70lb respectively.

Portugal
295 Perdigueiro Português

This Portuguese gundog is probably descended from the Italian bracco (23) and the Spanish perdiguero de Burgos (119) but is of a somewhat lighter build than the latter. It resembles a cross between a pointer (127) and a Hungarian vizsla (229). The head is fairly broad with a moderately short and blunt muzzle, thin drooping ears and a tail which is normally docked to one third of its natural length. The coat is short and coarse and of a golden Brown colour, which is darker on the head. Height at shoulder is 22in for dogs, 21in for bitches, but this may vary an inch or so either way.

296 Perro de Pastor Catalan

The Catalan herder, like its Portuguese counterpart, bears quite a close resemblance to the internationally better known bearded collie (41). The Spanish breed, however, has amber-coloured eyes and its tail may be either long and carried low or short—to a maximum of 4in. The coat is long and wavy, the colour a mixture of black and white with cream-coloured legs and feet.

Height at shoulder for dogs is 18–20in, 17–19in for bitches. The average weight is 40lb and 35lb respectively.

Spain
297 Perro de Presa Mallorquin

The perro de Presa Mallorquin is clearly of bulldog type and, in its original home area of the Balearic Islands, is highly valued as a guard dog. It has the massive and broad head of the bulldog (28) with the small, thin 'rose' ears and the wide, low-slung chest. It is, however, longer in the neck, and the tail is long and carried in a slight curve. The coat is short, brindle and without white markings.

Height at shoulder is about 23in.

Portugal
298 Podengo Português

The Portuguese podengo (not to be confused with the Spanish Ibizan hound, the podenco Ibicenco) is divided into three types: large, medium and toy. The breed is used primarily for rabbiting and the largest of the three varieties is used to course hare. The breed carries quite a lot of blood from various rough sighthound types. The largest variety has a conformation similar to that of a coarse Ibizan hound (126); the smallest variety has an affinity to the chihuahua (36).

The podengo has a pointed foreface, well defined stop and large, erect and mobile ears. The tail is of medium length, thick, and is often carried absolutely straight up, or slightly over the back. The coat may be smooth or wire-haired. The most common colour is fawn.

Height at shoulder for the largest podengo variety is 22–28in; 16–22in for the medium-sized variety and 8–12in for the toy.

France
299 Poitevin

The Poitevin is descended from now extinct French hounds and evolved during the latter half of the eighteenth century. Subsequently the English foxhound (58) was introduced into the breed and the Poitevin today bears quite a strong resemblance to its British relative. However, the ears are longer and thinner and the colour is usually black with orange and white—sometimes only white and orange.

Height at shoulder is 24–28in, weight around 66lb.

France
300 Porcelaine

Both the Swiss and the French regard the porcelaine as 'their' breed; however, it is officially recognised as French. It has been in existence since the end of the eighteenth century and is regularly used as a tracking/driving hound in France. Older French hounds and the English harrier are reputed to form the background of today's porcelaine.

It gets its name from its smooth, white and glossy coat, which is often decorated with small orange markings which are especially profuse on the ears. The head is long and well chiselled, and the eyes dark. The ears are long, set fairly high and fall in graceful folds. The tail is of medium length and is carried in a slight curve.

Height at shoulder varies between 22–23in for dogs, 21–22in for bitches.

Portugal
301 Rafeiro do Alentejo

The Portuguese herding dog originates from the province of Alentejo, south of Lisbon. It resembles the smooth St Bernard (143) but is lighter in build overall. The head is bear-like with a broad skull and small, dark eyes with a calm expression. Its medium-sized, dropped ears are very mobile. The tail is slightly curved and is carried curled into a ring when the dog is in action. The

298 Podengo Português

302 Rastreador Brasileiro

299 Poitevin

303 Sabueso Español

300 Porcelaine

304 Sar Planina

301 Rafeiro do Alentejo

305 Segugio Italiano

306 Steinbracke

311 Volpino Italiano

307 Steirischer Rauhaariger Hochgebirgsbracke

312 Xoloitzcuintle

308 Tibetan Mastiff

313 Österreichischer Bracke, Brandlbracke

309 Tiroler Bracke

314 Österreichischer Kurzhaariger Pinscher

coat is of medium length or short.

Acceptable colours are black, grey, cream or fawn with white markings. White with markings in any of these colours, or brindle, also occur. Height at shoulder is 26–29in for dogs, 25–28in for bitches.

Brazil
302 Rastreador Brasileiro

The Brazilian hound, the rastreador, is the result of interbreeding between the American foxhound (237) and the coonhound (43 and 44), among others. It is considered to be extremely hardy with great stamina and, even in the taxing climate of its home country, it is said to be able to trail its prey for hours in very difficult terrain.

It has a triangular, fairly long head with long, pendulous ears, dark eyes, a sabre-shaped tail and a short, close coat. The colour may be blue merle, white with black or tan patches, or black and tan. Height at shoulder is about 26in for dogs, slightly less for bitches.

Spain
303 Sabueso Español

This Spanish hound breed is thought to be several hundred years old. In addition to tracking game or driving it to the guns, it is used as a guard and police dog. There are two types: the common and the smaller. Both are broad and heavy in the head, with light or dark chestnut-coloured eyes, very long ears and a tail carried in a slight downward curve when the dog is at rest.

The colour is white with large patches in orange and black. Height at shoulder for the common sabueso Español is 20–22in for dogs, 19–20in for bitches. The smaller variety should not exceed 20in and 19in respectively.

Yugoslavia
304 Sar Planina

For centuries, the Sar Planina has been used as a herder in the Yugoslavian mountain areas. It is rarely seen at dog shows, but the local strains are jealously protected from any intermingling with strange blood.

The Sar Planina is regarded as a surviving link between the old Molossian dogs and the modern pastoral breeds. In conformation it resembles the hovawart (77). The head is slightly convex in profile with a hardly perceptible stop, a long powerful foreface and dark oval eyes. The ears are of medium size and dropped and the tail is set high and carried in an upward curve (it is occasionally docked). The coat is thick and abundant, shorter on the head and legs, but particularly profuse on the tail.

The colour is wolf grey, possibly with some white on the legs or the chest. Height at shoulder is about 22–23in.

Italy
305 Segugio Italiano

The Italian segugio is related to the northern European breeds of foxhound/harrier type, but is considerably more elegant. It has the air of the greyhound about it, but this impression is offset by its long, thin, pendulous ears, which hang in graceful folds. The head is long and fairly narrow, the bridge of the nose is slightly convex and the eyes are dark ochre in colour. The tail is thin and gracefully carried in a sabre-shaped curve. There are smooth-haired and wire-haired varieties.

The colour is a red fawn in various shades or black and tan. Height at shoulder is 21–23in for dogs, 19–22in for bitches.

Germany
306 Steinbracke

The steinbracke is less common than most other breeds within the 'bracke' group and the official breed standard is very brief. In comparison with, for example, the Westfälischer dachsbracke (264), the steinbracke is longer in the leg and more square in outline. The head is long and light and the eyes are clear with dark irises. The large ears are set high and lie flat against the head. The tail is set high and has a tuft of coarse hair at the tip. The coat is fairly short and close.

The colour is always tricolour. The breed is described as being of 'medium size', but no height at shoulder is specified in the breed standard.

307 Steirischer Rauhaariger Hochgebirgsbracke

The main difference between this variety of 'bracke' and the more common German ones is that the Austrian variety is wire-haired and slightly higher in the leg. It is very muscular and powerfully built with well developed sporting instincts. The eyes may be dark brown or yellow, the ears are dopped and, as distinct from the rest of the body, are covered with short, soft hair. The tail is curved sabre-fashion with a tuft of hair at the tip. The coat is wiry and bushy.

The colour is red or pale fawn, sometimes with a small white spot on the chest. Height at shoulder is 16–20in.

Great Britain
308 Tibetan Mastiff

Although, according to the International Canine Federation, the FCI, the Tibetan mastiff is officially regarded as a British breed, it is truly a product of the Central Asian plains. It is said to be still used in its country of origin as a guard of flocks of sheep and cattle. It is a very large and heavy breed, and bears a close resemblance to the St Bernard (143) with small ears carried close to a deep and broad skull. The eyes are deeply set and brown, the tail is set high and carried curled over the back. The coat is thick, with profuse feathering on the tail.

The colour should be black and tan or golden, but pure black is also acceptable. Height at shoulder is 25–27in for dogs, 22–24in for bitches.

Austria
309 Tiroler Bracke

The Tyrolean bracke is descended from a variety of local breeds and is used in its home country for various types of hunting according to the terrain. There are two types: the larger and smaller. The head is long and lightly boned with large, high-set and pendulous ears. The eyes are large with chestnut-brown irises. The occiput is pronounced, especially in dogs. The tail is long and slightly curved. The coat is short.

The basic colour is black, red or fawn, Small white markings are acceptable, as is tricolour. Height at shoulder is 16–19in for the larger variety, 12–15in for the smaller.

Great Britain
310 Trail Hound

The trail hound, which has no official breed standard, is basically a foxhound (58) which has been used for generations in the North of England for one particular purpose: taking part in trailing competitions over courses of several miles. Over the years the foxhound has been crossed with sighthounds and pointers to develop qualities of speed and agility to enable it to perform well in these trailing competitions.

It is not internationally recognised as a breed. A typical trail hound, however, is all sinew and muscle with every rib and vertebra showing through the skin. The coat, naturally short, is shaved before competitions. Most colours are acceptable and the most common are black and white, fawn or grey-and-white particolour.

Height at shoulder varies considerably—22–26in is about average.

Italy
311 Volpino Italiano

This little Italian spitz resembles the more common Pomeranian (128), but the ears are larger and more pointed and the foreface is longer. It has, reputedly, existed in Italy for several centuries. The coat is long and abundant with a thick undercoat. The colour is always white or red without markings; however, champagne-coloured dogs with faint orange markings on the ears are acceptable.

Height at shoulder is 11–12in for dogs, 10–11in for bitches.

Mexico
312 Xoloitzcuintle

The Mexican hairless dog has much in common with the equally rare

Chinese crested dog (37). However, it is much larger and has a smaller tuft of hair on the head than the Chinese breed. Hairless dogs have existed in Mexico since the beginning of recorded history; today they are almost as rare in their home country as abroad.

In conformation, the Mexican hairless resembles the Pinscher (123). It has a longish head with dark or yellow eyes. The ears are large and erect, the tail long and thin with a tuft at the end. With the exception of this and a sparse top-knot on the top of the skull, the dog is completely hairless and, as distinct from other breeds, perspires through the skin.

The most desirable colours are dark bronze brown, elephant grey or black, but a mixture of brown and flesh-coloured patches is also acceptable. Minimum height at shoulder is 12in, but around 20in is average.

Austria
313 Österreichischer Bracke, Brandlbracke

The Austrian brandlbracke has been given its name because of the flame-coloured markings in the black coat. It is extensively used for hunting in its home country but is almost completely unknown outside Austria. It is rectangular in body shape, the head is long and the eyes usually chestnut brown. The ears are moderately large, rounded at the tips and carried dropped. The tail is long, and the coat smooth and glossy.

The colour may be either black with flame-coloured markings or self-coloured red, possibly with a small white spot on the chest. Height at shoulder is 18–21in.

Austria
314 Österreichischer Kurz-haariger Pinscher

The Austrian short-haired pinscher is a 'young' breed and is still fairly unsettled in type and size—it can, for instance, range in height from just above miniature pinscher size to an inch or so taller than the pinscher (123 and 124). Several ear carriages are acceptable (dropped, erect or 'rose' ears) but semi-erect ears are considered most desirable. The tail may be either docked or carried over the back (when it should have bushy feathering). The coat is always short, but not necessarily completely smooth.

The colour is usually fawn, golden, deer red or black and tan—often with brindle markings. White markings on the muzzle, neck, chest and feet are quite common and acceptable. Height varies between 13–19in.

Appendix

315 Argentinian Mastiff
(Douge d'Argentine)

Even in classical antiquity there existed large dogs of mastiff type in the northern Mediterranean countries, called Molossian dogs. These dogs were named after the Molossians, a tribe that came from the east and who invaded north western Greece in about 500BC, claiming these dogs as part of their war booty. This type of dog then spread westwards and eventually became established in north-west Spain and Portugal.

The Argentinian mastiff is descended from those Molossian dogs which came to South America with Spanish settlers in the sixteenth century. They were used as shepherds and guards and as hunters of big game. They even had to serve as battle dogs in the not infrequent skirmishes between rival colonies.

The Argentinian mastiff is a medium-sized, sturdy and muscular dog of distinct bull-breed type. The ears should be cropped to triangular shape; the neck is strong with plenty of loose skin as in the bulldog, the chest is broad, the back strong and the hindquarters well developed. The tail should not be docked and is carried high when the dog is excited. The coat is short, dense and hard. The only permissible colour is all white, and any other markings are a disqualifying fault.

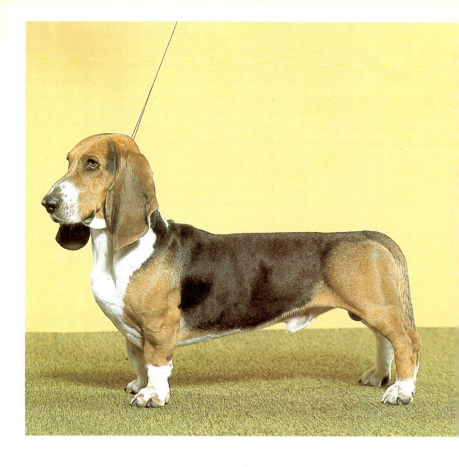

316 Basset Artésien-Normand

The French equivalent of the German dachshund is the basset, which comes in many varieties. Like the dachshund, it has evolved due to a mutation, ie a sudden change in the genetic make-up, which has then been fixed as a characteristic through selective breeding. In this case the short, crooked legs are really due to a congenital defect (chondrodystrophy) which affects the formation of bone from cartilage, halting the growth process of the bone earlier than is normal. In the German dachshund this trait has been gradually bred out, but this is not so in the basset Artésien-Normand. On the contrary, straight legs are regarded as a disqualifying fault. As the crooked legs put great pressure on joints and ligaments, especially when the dog is hunting, it must be considered both irrational and cruel to keep deformed legs as a desirable feature in such an active hound as the basset Artésien-Normand.

Like the other basset varieties, the basset Artésien-Normand is long and low. It should be robust, yet not lacking in style. The coast is short and smooth, the colour either tricolour (black, white and tan) or white with orange markings. Height at shoulder is about 10–14in.

Switzerland
317 Bernese Laufhund
(Berner Laufhund)

The Swiss harriers, the laufhunde, have a very long history and we have been able to follow their development over the centuries in art and literature. They were first depicted in the eleventh century and irrefutable evidence of their existence has been found in documents and paintings from both the fifteenth and the seventeenth centuries.

Towards the end of the nineteenth century, interest in the native harrier breeds decreased both in Switzerland and in Germany as imported breeds came into fashion. The local types were, however, saved from extinction through the dedicated work of some enthusiastic breeders.

There are eight varieties of Swiss harrier: the Bernese laufhund, the Jura laufhund (bruno de Jura 27), the Lucerne laufhund (96), the Swiss laufhund (150) and the miniature varieties of these four breeds, the niederlaufhunde (290–293).

The Bernese laufhund is a rectangularly-built dog of medium size. The coat is short, smooth and dense. The colour is tricolour, ie white with black patches and tan markings on the head, the white sometimes being intermingled with a profusion of small black spots. Height at shoulder for dogs should be 20–22in, for bitches 19–21in. The miniature varieties were bred down to size (12–15in) when the Swiss imposed a ban on hunting with tracking/driving dogs higher than 17½in at shoulder.

318 Griffon Bleu de Gascogne

It is not known how the griffon group of breeds got its name. The word 'griffon' is either derived from the Latin 'gryphus' or from the German 'griffer' or 'greiffer', ie seizing, grabbing. On the Continent, it has come to represent a group of wire-haired hunting dogs of harrier type. The griffons are still wire-haired, though they are not all hunting dogs today. One exception is the Belgian toy dog, the griffon Bruxellois.

There are two varieties in size of the griffon bleu de Gascogne. The larger variety, the grand griffon bleu de Gascogne, resembles another French harrier, the Billy (244), but it has a wrinkled forehead and long, low set ears. The coat is of medium length, fairly thick and very harsh. The colour is white intermingled with small black spots giving a speckled blue shade, hence the name. Height at shoulder for dogs is 25–28in, for bitches 24–26in.

The photograph shows the smaller variety, the griffon bleu de Gascogne de petit taille, which in everything but size is a copy of its larger relative. It has flat, dropped ears and a slightly curved tail. The colour is the same as in the grand griffon bleu de Gascogne, but height at shoulder should not exceed 17–21in.

319 Iceland Spitz (Islandshund)

It has been said that the people living in a belt around the North Pole have their own breed of dog as a national symbol. The Iceland spitz is the only breed to have evolved on the island and it has existed there for more than a thousand years.

As its name implies, the Iceland spitz belongs to the spitz breeds which were the first known dogs on the Scandinavian peninsula. Archaeological finds have shown that the dogs of the Stone Age people were of spitz type. The oldest remains of dogs found in Scandinavia—some skulls dating from late Stone Age —show a great likeness to the head shape of the spitz today.

Some of these ancient spitz came to Iceland around the year 800AD with the first Norwegian immigrants. There they became the ancestors of the present Iceland spitz, in the same way as they fathered the elkhound (108) and the Norwegian buhund (107) in Norway.

Like other spitz breeds, the Iceland spitz has a wedge-shaped head, erect ears and a tail curled over the back. The coat is of medium length and harsh; colour is white with cream markings, or golden or cream with black tips. Height at shoulder is 15–18in.

320 Lakenois

Towards the end of the nineteenth century most western European countries took a new interest in their native shepherd breeds. In many places the local varieties of shepherd dog differed from one another so little that it was decided to try to amalgamate them into one breed. In Germany these efforts produced the German shepherd dog (Alsatian, 47), whereas in Belgium virtually the same foundation stock – the original German and Belgian herding dogs were very similar in type – resulted in eight varieties of the Belgian shepherd: three long-haired, two short-haired and three wire-haired varieties.

This classification into so many varieties made breeding more difficult as it limited the selection of stud dogs and brood bitches. However, in 1897 it was decided to reduce the varieties to four: the two long-haired varieties, the Groenendael (71) and the Tervueren (226), the short-haired malinois (98) and the wire-haired lakenois.

Apart from coat texture and colour, the lakenois is virtually a copy of its long-haired and short-haired cousins. The coat should be double: a soft and woolly undercoat and a harsh and wiry top coat. The colour is tan with faint black shadings. Height at shoulder for dogs is 24in, for bitches 23in.

321 Shar Pei

The Chinese breed shar pei is several hundred years old. It is mostly found in the coastal regions of the South China Sea. It is said to originate from the town Dah Let in the province of Kwun Tung. It was originally used for hunting wild boar or at arranged dog fights, which at one time were a popular pastime in China as well as in England and in the USA. In England this 'sport' was introduced when bull baiting (fights between bull and dog) was abolished by law in 1835.

The shar pei is a dog of medium size with a sturdy, compact body. It has a calm and friendly temperament. Its most characteristic feature is the very loose skin which makes the shar pei the most wrinkled of breeds. The coat is short, bristly and very hard. The colour is black, red or brown in different shades, or cream, slightly lighter on the back of the thighs and underneath the tail. White markings are not acceptable. Height at shoulder is 16–20in.

In recent years the shar pei has been exported to the USA. There are also a few specimens in Denmark.

322 Russian Black Terrier

Despite its name, the black terrier is not an old Russian breed, neither is it a terrier. It looks like a mixture of the giant schnauzer (148) and the bouvier (21), and is likely to have evolved through crosses between these and other western European breeds brought into Russia. It is possible that one of its ancestors may be a native Russian breed which has long since ceased to leave its mark on its breed type.

The black terrier is over medium size, strongly built with good bone and well muscled. A characteristic of the breed is that it is reserved towards strangers, yet without being aggressive. It is very hardy and adjusts easily to different types of climate and environment. It is also easy to train. The difference between the sexes is clearly marked, the dog being heavier and more compact than the bitch.

The coat is dense and slightly wavy but must not be curly or hanging flat. The top coat is harsh, dense and tight, the undercoat profuse. Other features are a hard bristly moustache, harsh whiskers and prominent eyebrows. The colour is black or dark grey. Height at shoulder for dogs is 26–28in, 25–27in for bitches.

Index

The numbers in this index refer to the corresponding numbers of text and illustrations.